CHEWING GUM UNDER THE TABLE

A travel story that will leave you
wanting to buy a bus

PAULINE GRAVES

CHEWING GUM UNDER THE TABLE

PREFACE

Memories fade as we get older and I did not want my two children to ever forget the amazing adventure we had touring America on a bus. So, this book and the short stories in it are for Jake and Josh and of course anyone else who is interested.

PROLOGUE

Where would we be without our dreams and visions? But how often do they come true? As often as we make them? Is it luck? Determination? Bloody mindedness? Or even pure hard work? Perhaps it's a bit of everything.

My thoughts now are in Hong Kong remembering with clarity one evening with Keith when an idea came into our minds. We had just finished the bedtime routine with our two-year-old son Jake. A fun bath followed by a bedtime story and then looking down at the now sleeping Jake, a contented smile on his face, and a mop of black hair on the pillow. The conversation was lively between us as it was this precise day that we had received confirmation from the Hong Kong Social Welfare Department that our application for a second child had been successful. In practice this meant a patient wait of six to nine months before being told precisely who our new child was to be. Before too long Jake would have a brother and our family plans would be fulfilled. With Josh now a twinkling in our eyes and all the adoption procedure soon to be behind us, we looked to the future. Our inspiration came from friends Harry and Carol who had for a few years been travelling the world by bus and later a purpose-built Winnebago. With their adventures in mind it occurred to us that it would be great to take some time out with our family and travel to maybe Australia, or Europe or even America by coach. The Graves family takes to the road, how Bohemian. We really were warming to this idea.

It was not long after this we did a three-week home and car exchange with Mike and Karen from Florida. It was to be Jake's first holiday. Driving around Florida we couldn't help but notice all the rather large coaches we were passing. In reality these are what the Americans call Recreational Vehicles or RVs for short. They use the expression camping when on holiday with these huge luxurious vehicles but let's be clear, this is a long way away from hammering pegs into the ground, sleeping on ground sheets and queuing up with washing up bowls. The Americans have been "camping" this way long before the word 'glamping' became holiday vocabulary.

It didn't take us long before our curiosity got the better of us and we found ourselves in one of Florida's many RV dealers' showrooms. Being British we are used to caravans and campervans. My early childhood memories of caravanning conjure up smells of breakfast bacon cooking, cramped spaces and rainy days. I remember Mum and Dad laboriously having to take out the beds at night and add the bedding and then fold them away again in the morning to form seats and a dining table. With this in mind it is understandable why I was stunned when I first entered one of these remarkable vehicles. We were less than upfront with the sales lady, who incidentally was named ET, and who was a lovely all-American lady who clearly wanted to impress in the hope it would eventually lead to a sale. She started off by showing us a top of the range model, no doubt with a view to working down to more affordable models. What a luxury: thick soft carpets, carved wooden surrounds, soft leather upholstery, an American-style fridge, stunning bathroom facilities, home study area, king size bed. Most impressive was the washer and dryer attached to the back of the coach and there was something we had never imagined. Slides. These slides led me to show my ignorance to ET. I knew the walls included sliders to expand and contract the RV's interior space, but the thought that every time you parked the coach ready for the evening it was necessary to manually yank these very heavy sliders out and then in the morning yank them back in was rather off-putting. Hard manual labour was not my idea of fun. I shared these thoughts with ET, who knowingly smiled at this British clown standing before her. She turned her head, reached to press a button and the large slider quietly, slowly, and efficiently "slid" shrinking the room by over a metre. I guess I had a lot to learn about RVing and I would welcome the chance with open arms.

I think it was that day the dream was born, a dream that was to be fulfilled and one we would all remember, hopefully forever.

THE INCIDENT AT THE US EMBASSY, BANGKOK

It's funny, but as parents we sometimes put our children into the most unnatural situations and expect them to shine, rising to the task as though a magic spell had been cast. For example, just occasionally we want them to behave as adults, we do not want them to embarrass us, and we would like, if possible, for them to follow behind us, say nothing, and do exactly as we tell them.

The trip to the US embassy in Bangkok was one of those times. We were there to apply for visas, which are usually granted to UK nationals for six months. We were going to be cheeky and ask for a one-year visa, not knowing if there was such a concession. I guessed if we were lucky, we would be at the Embassy for around one and a half hours; if we were unlucky it would be more like three to four hours. This belief came from embassy horror stories our friends had told from time to time. Therefore, I came prepared, as most mums do, with the usual Mary Poppins bag with contents enough to see us through a long siege.

Keith had also come fully prepared. He had spent hours laboriously filling out the necessary forms online and printing out barcodes which, in theory, should save us the long queues.

It did not, of course, because on the day we chose to visit, the Embassy's computer system wasn't working properly and couldn't recognize any of the printed barcodes. This meant we had to start from scratch, and from the back of the queue. Where else?

The frustration of having to collect a whole new set of forms and instruction booklets, pens, erasers, something to lean on and somewhere to sit and write, still annoys me to this day, but after about two and a half hours I was beginning to think that someone really had waved that magic wand over the boys, or should I say angels. My fears of being denied visas because of out of control children were fading. How proud we were amongst other parents, who were smiling jealously through their teeth, while their children were noisily misbehaving. It was at this time that we were advised to wait for another half hour, or until our names were called for the all-important interview.

The angels began to fidget for the first time. Eyeing up a drinks machine they wondered if they could buy a coke. Why not indeed after such exemplary behaviour. Off they trotted with their Thai Baht coins. The drinks machine was quite a way away but just in our vision, and there they stayed happily playing for about forty-five minutes until our name was called.

Keith approached the desk while I rustled up the boys. The couple in front of us had just been refused their visas so we began to be a bit nervous. The immigration officer directed her questions individually at us, including the boys, wanting to know a lot of background information. It was at this point, whilst Josh was answering a question, that I happened to notice his trousers were hanging heavily round his hips, Rasta style, and bulging rather unnaturally at the sides. As I didn't like the look of the vision in front of me and didn't like where my thoughts were leading, I decided to ignore the problem for the time being. From behind Jake's slim silhouette a similar bulge was to be seen at both sides where his pockets were. At this point I remember smiling at the officer, red-faced. After more questions we were granted a six month visa, for which we were very grateful. Shuffling our way out, trying hard to avoid the security cameras, ignoring the sound of coins jangling from the vicinity of their pockets, not daring to question the boys for fear of being seen on CCTV camera on "US soil", we eventually got to the bottom of why their pockets were stuffed full. "Well, it was easy, Mum, for every five Baht coin we put in the machine we got two five baht coins back instead of a drink, so we kept them!" Josh was so pleased with himself, loving the idea of making money. Jake too was smiling contentedly, although a little red-faced. I often wonder if that machine ever got fixed.

BUYING A COACH

There I was, not a care in the world, relaxing around a pool at my favourite time of day, late afternoon, when the harsh burn of the sun is gone and all that's left is the pleasant warmth of the coming evening, and the tempting prospect of a glass of cold white wine. I was in Xemxia, Malta, the pool was our hotel pool, and a feeling of contentment was washing over me. Today we had signed an agreement to purchase a Maltese house, and now I felt as if relaxing for a few minutes was well deserved. I was happy in the knowledge that all our plans were now coming together. The boys were having the greatest time in the pool with their newly found friends who included crocodiles and whales. All was well, until a mother of one of these new friends, meaning to be sociable, asked Josh where he lived. Most guests had left the pool area to prepare for the evening's entertainment and it was quiet enough for me to hear the conversation. It was a simple question. Josh of course thinking about it carefully, answered clearly and truthfully. "Oh," he said, "we don't have a home anymore, we're homeless!" With ten sets of eyes now boring into me, the enormity of our decision to travel around America in a coach with two relatively young children hit me.

The word "homeless" had made me realize the size of the adventure we were undertaking. Within the space of two weeks we had bought a house, applied for planning permission, and employed an architect and builder. Tomorrow we were getting on a plane towards the USA to live on a bus. Several people were looking at me expecting an explanation for my son's use of the word homeless but I couldn't give one. I smiled sweetly and sat it out.

Not long after this, having paused for breath with a few days with Nana in England, we arrived in Tampa, Florida. Any negative feelings, all long gone, were replaced with huge excitement. We were on our way! Having just rented a car it was now time to rectify our homeless situation. We checked in at a Country Inns and Suites Hotel, which was to be our home for a week or two, or until we purchased our coach. The hotel was chosen for its location as it was within walking distance of the RV dealer "Lazy Days". The boys grew to love this temporary home for reasons which were food-related. Josh because his favourite crispy bacon was on offer every breakfast time. The type of bacon that is so processed it can walk to the microwave by itself, and only needs twenty seconds to cook. Nevertheless, it is still delicious. The lady running the buffet, taken with the English accent, big eyes, and cute smile, was more than happy to accommodate him with a fresh tray daily. Josh was fast learning how to work a room. Jake loved this new home because at any time of the day there were always fresh cookies available when walking through the reception area, and because these were complimentary it seemed to hold even more attraction. I have to say the oversized, over chocolatey, over chewy cookies were rather good.

When one mentions dealers, in particular of vehicles, it's very easy to conjure up in your mind seedy dealings with seedy people with dirty fingernails, whom you wouldn't bring home and introduce to your mother. I have to say that with this in my mind, along with the dreaded thought of having to endure at least a few days of the infamous hard sell was quite daunting, and I guess I was arming myself emotionally for a tough day. The company itself, Lazy Days, was recommended to us by our friends, who had had dealings with them several years before. The reason they spoke so highly was related to their after-sales service, which we were told was second to none.

As we made our way from our hotel to Lazy Days reception, we walked through the campground. It became clear that this was a very together Company. The campground alone housing a large pool and hot tub, all enclosed in a lanai. There were high standard shower facilities, tennis courts, two restaurants, a shop, wi-fi, internet and more. There were over three hundred camping sites, which from now on I will call "Hook-ups". These were all spread over a large parkland area. Hook-up because they all have 30 or 50 amp electric power, mains water, and mains drainage to attach to each coach. Rubbish collection was twice daily.

When we arrived at the sales offices it was clear my first thoughts were very wrong. This was no seedy outfit employing dirty finger nailed, over aftershaved, shiny-suited sales staff. This was a highly sophisticated, professional business. Even the hard sell was notably subtle. We were told of the one hundred and twenty six acres of oak tree canopied property, full of many varied types of RV. We were also told of the two hundred and twenty service bays staffed by numerous expert technicians. In fact, they lived up to their advertised one-stop shop. Sales, finance, insurance, service and parts, and free breakfasts if you were a potential customer or staying on their campsite.

In a way it was easy for us because we knew exactly what we were looking for, having spent hours searching online. We wanted to purchase a coach with a so-called bunkhouse layout. This is simply a vehicle with permanent bunk beds very suitable for children, in addition to a separate bedroom with a fixed king-size bed for the parents. We knew that, whilst not unknown, they were at that time hard to locate. The sales executive promised they could have one or two even three for us to look at within two weeks, but in the meantime we were welcome to have a look through the vast assortment of stock on site, just in case we changed our minds. We enjoyed doing this for a day but we needed to be firm. We were looking to close a deal within the week.

Over the next few days we visited many dealers all within the Tampa area without much success. We eventually cast our net wider and noticed a very tall road sign advertising the name North Trail R V Centre outside of Fort Myers, well south of Tampa. A brilliant find, as this was another very large R V dealer boasting to be South Florida's largest, as well as being award-winning. I have to say most of the awards seemed to come from their suppliers. As soon as we arrived we were approached by friendly Kevin, who suggested we took our time to investigate the massive stock they were carrying. About fifty million USD we were told. We took him a little bit by surprise when he realized that not only did we know what we were looking for, but we were looking to close the correct deal as soon as we could. We were not tyre kickers. This would save him a lot of time and hard sell, which meant of course that we had his full attention. It didn't take him long to show us the Newmar Bay Star model which we eventually bought. This was without a doubt love at first sight. It was just perfect. Not too big and not too small. Complete with bunk beds, king size bed, bathroom, dining area, kitchen and lounge. What more could we need? "Yes, we will take this one," we told Kevin who nearly fell off his chair. From the time we arrived there, to the time it took us to make our decision, it was under an hour, and it was clear that Kevin was impressed. However, there was a problem: it was already sold, or so he thought. After checking with the boss we discovered it had been sold with a premise, the customer concerned was still waiting for finance and needed it to be approved, therefore the sales team were free to sell it. I have to say we were all very pleased, the boys having already sorted out who was sleeping on which bunk, and where their clothes were going.

Keith and I were then whisked off to see the accountant and the Boss for payment procedures, and the two boys followed Kevin who assured us he just loved children. I guess this must be one of the major disadvantages of Kevin's line of work. The paperwork that followed was quite laborious, even complicated, and took about ninety minutes to complete. Making payment, buying insurance. Registering the vehicle in our names at our US Houston "home address", buying extra tyre insurance and so on. When we saw Kevin again he was knee-deep in popcorn, playing games with the boys. We noticed there was a popcorn machine in the corner which was looking a bit sad and empty.

Luckily one thing we had considered earlier was that we needed a fixed address in America in order to register our new coach in our name and also to receive all our mail, official and otherwise. After some research we had found a company who we could register as our home address and who would receive all our mail and forward it to wherever we were. Thus our "home" address became Houston, Texas and the coach was registered in our name there and all our future post would be forwarded from there. Phew!!

So what had we actually bought? What is a Newmar Bay Star? Our coach was thirty four feet in length, Ford V10 Triton 6.8 litre gas engine, 6 speed auto gearbox, cruise control, Ford Chassis 20,500 lbs, with a gas tank that holds 75 US gallons. 10 US gallons = 8 UK gallons, or 284 litres. A family car holds around 40 litres. We were to expect, when towing, around 8 miles to the gallon. The spec also included Air-conditioning and heating and a 5500 capacity generator. The coach also had two slides which I'll talk about later. To top it off a propane gas tank to run the central heating and cooker hob.

North Trail are the largest dealers for Newmar and explained that all the interiors are made by the Amish people who are known for excellent workmanship, particularly cabinetry and carpentry, though they do have strange ideas about the number and ages of the wives the men are allowed, and prefer horse and carriage to cars.

The far end of the coach housed the master bedroom complete with king size bed, bedside tables, double wardrobe, cupboard space, vanity unit with mirror, and a 20" TV. There was a sliding door making this room quite private if need be. This led to the two single bunk beds. Underneath the bottom bunk were large storage drawers ideal for clothes. There was a ladder at the side for easy top bunk access. Almost opposite was the bathroom with shower, washbasin and toilet. The hallway led into the kitchen and dining area. A four-seater table with cushioned seats made the dining area. The kitchen consisted of a pantry, large fridge-freezer, microwave, three-ring gas hob and oven, double sink and draining boards, along with ample cupboard space. A three-seater sofa complete with underneath storage, a matching armchair, along with a 26" satellite television with automatic satellite searching, and a Sony surround sound home theatre made a comfortable lounge area. Both the driver and passenger seats in the cockpit were made to swivel around to make extra armchairs for the lounge.

I found the slides to be most fascinating. By pushing a button you made the space inside increase or decrease as the side of the coach moved outwards or back in. There was a slide to extend the master bedroom and one to extend the lounge area, only when parked of course. It was also important to remember to push forward the driver's seat before activating the lounge slide or it would rip the driver's seat off its moorings. The slides were amazing as they made a huge difference to our living areas.

We still had a few extras to buy and be fitted so we couldn't take Bay Star, as she had become known, away with us, but looked forward to returning the next day to organize things.

It was that evening over dinner we discovered something which confirmed our children as typical boys. We had been in America for one week and both Jake and Josh had their favourite restaurants, namely The Cracker-Barrel Restaurant and Country Store, and Bob Evans. I have to say these were perhaps the best of the bunch in the area. We were in Bob Evans that night and I couldn't work out why the boys, when seated at the table, insisted in ducking underneath for a few seconds and popping back up giggling, saying to each other a number to see who had won. "Well, Mum, in America everyone chews gum, and there are no gum trays so they stick their chewing gum underneath the table, but some people forget to collect it when they leave. We've been having a competition to see who can find the most. Today I spotted 12 pieces and I won." I often wonder if girls would share the same fascination for such unwholesome topics. I must make a mental note to check under my dining room table.

Next day we returned to North Trail to address another unwholesome topic. The travelling sewage system. Most coaches are designed to house a basic system that is adequate, but for us this wasn't good enough. We imagined all sorts of unpleasant scenarios with shades of Robin Williams in his film RV. We had to have the latest state of the art system newly on the market. Keith really outsourced himself here. As there is no genteel way to describe the workings of such a system I'll come straight to the point. Imagine a kitchen whirly waste, where all the kitchen waste gets churned together by a rather loud machine with lots of blades. Eventually these waste products form a smooth paste which then goes through a pipe later to be transported to the sewers. Well, that's it in a nutshell but not for the kitchen, instead for the loo. This system came with a guarantee not to leak. We shall see.

Another system we added to our coach was reverse osmosis drinking water. There are three water tanks on the coach: the white tank, this is clean water used for showering and kitchen use and for drinking, having gone through reverse osmosis system. This tank needs filling up with water. The grey tank holds the water that has already been used for showering and kitchen use. This tank requires emptying. Then there is the Black tank; this is sewage. So the reverse osmosis system was attached under the sink in the kitchen to the white tank. The black tank is attached to the aforementioned whirly wastey thingy and definitely needs frequent emptying.

Fitting the sewage and reverse osmosis systems would take about two days. This would give us enough time to ditch our rental car and buy our tow car or "Toad" as the locals call it. A Toad would be needed for sightseeing and for basic everyday shopping to avoid taking a thirty-four foot coach to the supermarket. We found a car showroom district and began our search for a suitable vehicle, each one of us having a particular car in mind. I am still not sure where my thoughts were at the time, but I remember thinking practical things like large boot, plenty of leg room, cup holders and such things. I saw the exact car for us, a Blue Saturn, it ticked every box including price and the fact that Saturns can be towed with four wheels on the ground. I discovered you can't do this with too many vehicles because of some strange gearbox technology. At the time I couldn't understand the reaction from all three boys; Josh just plainly didn't like it, Jake threatened never to get in it, and Keith was just speechless. It wasn't until much later I realized just how ugly and low down this car was. It was certainly not the image that would fit into our now new bohemian nomad lifestyle. I could see that I had quite blotted my copy book, so feeling in total disgrace I handed the job of sourcing our Toad to Keith, Jake and Josh.

It didn't take them long to discover what we affectionately got to know as Tobie. Tobie was a Jeep, two litre engine, stick shift, four wheel drive, and rag top. Translated into English, manual gear box with a soft top. Named Tobie simply because her purpose was to be towed.

I must also add, that Tobie had very little boot space, hardly space for two bags of shopping, very little room inside, a leaky soft top and definitely no cup holders; however, this was the vehicle that almost everyone was excited about, so we decided to buy it. It was now that we encountered that stereotype seedy salesman, except that he was in disguise. Youthful, trendy clothes, cool speech which I found to be not quite corny, but his fingernails along with his insincere smile and shifty eyes told a different story. This certainly was no character for anyone's mother to meet.

It was then I realized just how much the boys wanted this Jeep. When I suggested we should walk away and find another more reliable Jeep dealer their looks threatened to put me back into disgrace. I did stand my ground though, washed my hands of this whole transaction and simply let them get on with it. The man promised to fit a new fuel pump ready for the next day.

In the meantime, we had a lot of shopping to attend to, a new home to kit out. How exciting. We decided Ikea was probably the best option as we considered this to be a one-stop shop and Ikea has the reputation of being economical. Our list seemed huge. Bedding, towels, kitchen utensils, cook pots including a kettle, crockery – actually the list doesn't seem so big now, but it only just fitted into the rental car, which incidentally had a huge boot. The boys just disappeared under quilts, pillows and sheets in the back, but we made it back to the hotel in one piece. The receptionist wasn't too sure about us hillbillies unloading all of our worldly goods into our room, but I guess she was well trained, so nothing was mentioned.

It actually took four days to fit the new fuel pump, but with that behind us we now had the job of returning to North Trail in Fort Myers, to select and fit the tow bar and drive the coach and Tobie, all hitched up, back to Lazy Days in Tampa, where we expected to stay for the next ten days or so familiarizing ourselves with coach living. As we arrived at the now familiar North Trail, Kevin was there to meet us with his usual smile; he noticed the Jeep and we both exchanged unsaid thoughts. Keith and Kevin got to work quickly selecting the appropriate tow bar and having it fitted onto the back of the coach. Kevin then proceeded to teach us both exactly how to hitch and unhitch Tobie to the coach – not easy at first but we gradually got the idea. The huge things to remember were that it would be silly to leave the handbrake on the Jeep when trying to pull it behind us, and also that the steering wheel must be unlocked otherwise Tobie would not follow us. This meant the ignition key must be in the slot and in the halfway position so the steering wheel, and therefore the wheels, would turn. I remember writing down all the instructions for future reference. Next came a teach in about the basic functions of the coach, how to work the various appliances, the air conditioning system, heating system, slides, generator, how to empty the grey and black water, how to refill the white water.

At last came the big lesson: driving the coach. Having previously agreed with Keith that he would drive the coach back the one hundred and twenty miles to Tampa I watched them both as they made their way to the coach so that Kevin could demonstrate just how easy it was to drive this mere thirty-four footer along the nearest country roads. This size is not considered particularly large by experienced RV'ers. I was a little shocked when they returned twenty minutes later with Keith supposedly having been fully briefed, but Kevin assured me there was nothing to it. So, there was nothing more to do but to find the children, say our goodbyes and get on our way.

You can imagine the excitement of this first ride, the boys choosing their seats, getting comfortable and seat belted up .We were all so excited, but Keith, I knew, would never admit to how nervous he really was. So, we were off, slowly, slowly, we left the parking lot and turned onto a main road which led eventually to the main highway. All was well, all we had to do was keep on this highway through Port Charlotte, Sarasota, Bradenton and then on to Tampa. If only Keith would go faster than twenty miles an hour we might get back in time for dinner. I noticed we had started to veer over to the left straddling the white line, driving on the wrong side of the road of course. I also noticed that there was a police car two cars behind us. In fact, it was really one car behind us because the car immediately behind us was Tobie. Silly me. At least she was still attached. Keith, I could see, was concentrating very hard, so I wasn't sure whether to mention the police; however, he had noticed, so I then gently suggested he should try and keep within the white lines – this wasn't at all easy, I was told. The boys picking up on the situation put on their sunglasses and began to practise their American FBI accents, or was it Hawaii Five O. The police stayed with us for another twenty miles and decided to move on to more lucrative things or so

I assumed. By this time Keith, gaining confidence, managed to pick up speed to a comfortable sixty miles an hour, just occasionally drifting over the white line.

When we arrived at Lazy Days, we were all exhausted, Keith deserved a medal or at least an icy cold beer, but not yet. We had to check in for a fourteen day stay, unattach Tobie, drive to our hook-up and reverse into it. So out came my notes on how to unhook a Toad. As the tow bar equipment was new it was very stiff, so this task initially proved to be very difficult; eventually we got there, or I should say Keith did. We said a quiet goodnight to Bay star and Tobie, and headed back to the hotel for our last night under bricks and mortar.

The next day we checked out of the hotel and moved into the coach. We had decided to spend fourteen days here basically to orientate ourselves to our new routines and general lifestyle. It took the whole day to move everything in and make things comfortable. After dinner that night the boys couldn't wait to get to their beds; Jake being the eldest took the top bunk, Josh the bottom. They looked so snug in their cotton sleeping bags and fluffy pillows. We too decided to have an early night as we wanted to try out the bedroom television system. After about an hour we said our goodnights as you do. Little did we know this was to become our nightly routine which stayed with us for a long time afterwards. It goes something like this:

Josh: Goodnight Mum

Mum: Goodnight Josh and sweet dreams.

Josh: Sweet dreams to you, Mum.

Dad: Goodnight Josh

Josh: Goodnight Dad, sweet dreams

Dad: Sweet dreams, Josh

Jake: Goodnight Mum… and so on and so on.

There were nights it seemed to go on forever, in no time at all we had become The Waltons on wheels.

The next day we planned together the following few days. Today would be taken up with food shopping and buying any items required for the boys' schooling such as exercise books and extra stationery essentials, because the following day home schooling was to begin.

The food shopping took a long time, as you would expect. American supermarkets were larger than any we had seen, and getting to know a quick way around an enormous food Walmart was going to take time. As you can imagine, our first shop, which was basically a starter food pack, was going to be a big one. We left the checkout with about ten carrier bags, and piled them into the Jeep. Of course they didn't fit, but the boys were going to have to get used to sharing their seats with many bags in-between and on their knees and under their armpits on such occasions. The Jeep was their choice, after all.

From a safety point of view, we had always considered taking an RV driving course and now we thought this could only be an advantage. In America an HGV licence is not a legal requirement unless the vehicle is over forty-four feet, but we decided to book our course with the famous Barney Alexander. This was due to take place in the afternoons. The course was in two parts over two days. We wouldn't leave the boys on their own so we booked in on separate days. This was something we were looking forward to in a few days' time.

We also decided that after the first section of home schooling, before we left Tampa, we would take a day out as a treat, so we began to plan a day at Busch Gardens.

But first things first. Prior to arriving in America, the concept of home schooling was discussed many times as a family, so the boys were well prepared and knew what to expect. The school started at nine o'clock. The boys were to be ready at this time, meaning all showers, breakfasts, bed making and tidying had to be completed by this time, along with making sure all their books and pencils were in order. This was a routine that we kept up all through the adventure. The teaching system was quite simple: Keith would take the Maths, myself the English. Given their age difference they were taught individually. The majority of the History, Geography or Humanities would take place outside in situ. For example, when we wanted to explain erosion in conjunction with the Grand Canyon we would just go and look at it. Appropriate projects were planned to cover certain topics.

The actual schooling conducted in the coach lasted until

twelve thirty. We would always start the day with something of local interest before commencing with the lessons. Keith and I would go through the following day's lesson plans the night before so we were ourselves organized.

The very first day we discussed the home school timetable, where the books were to be kept – which was outside in one of the numerous storage lockers – and our plans for that week, which was a general recap of their previous year's lessons. The boys labelled all their exercise books, selected some reading books, discussed future projects and began learning about Florida. We all learnt that Florida was nicknamed the sunshine state, that the orange blossom is the state flower and the mocking bird the state bird, that Tallahassee is the capital of Florida and that it has been a state since 1845. Later, similar basic facts were learnt for each state. Florida came alive when we went in search of the mocking bird and orange blossom. Josh was very interested in the Everglades, the bird life and of course the alligators. We promised a serious visit to the Everglades at the end of our trip on the way back. They both were interested in Cape Canaveral, which is where the John F Kennedy Space Center is. It was from this base that astronaut Alan Shepard became the first American in space in 1961, John Glenn became the first American to orbit the earth in 1962 and the famous Neil Armstrong became the first man to walk on the moon.

Because Jake, when we lived in Thailand, had followed

the US elections all the way through from the primaries, I understood his interest now in American politics. This was kept very much alive here in Florida mainly because Floridians loved to share their political point of view, and we loved their openness, which seemingly was more forthcoming when our foreign nationalities were discovered. Jake loved to listen to and even join in these conversations and he soon realized that many of the people we talked to were Republicans, and Republicans of course were against President Obama in a big way. Nevertheless, it was clear that these Floridians had stirred up an interest in Jake that was to last for some time. As we were coming to the end of this time in Florida, excitement was beginning to build up in us all. Very soon the next stage of our adventure would start and we were going to head for New Orleans. Couldn't wait.

Coach and Toad

The drivers

Slides out

THE DRIVING CONFIDENCE COURSE

I remember really looking forward to learning how to drive our RV, so it was with some excitement and enthusiasm that I arrived at the course venue. There was gathered a mix of people, mainly couples, who appeared to me rather elderly, although I never was much good at determining age. I sat eagerly awaiting the arrival of instructor Barney Alexander and making small talk with my fellow students. When he did arrive, he didn't disappoint.

We may love to criticize our Americans friends, bless them, as of course they do us; however, I do believe they make excellent teachers. They seem to be able to simplify matters in such a way that they can be understood by anybody. I long ago realized that simplification is just the end product of thoroughly understanding something highly complex. With this in mind I have only praise, and say three cheers for

America and Barney. He is a great teacher. In no time at all he held us all captivated. We were now putty in his hands for the next several hours.

The course was split over two days. Day one we were to study coach driving theory, and day two we would go out driving, putting all our new knowledge to the test.

First on the agenda. Adjusting the mirrors.

I thought I knew all about the mirrors, but was happy to find out more. There is a total of four huge mirrors, a set of two on each side. Each set contains a flat mirror and convex mirror. The flat mirror will pick up a following vehicle at distance, the convex mirror will pick up the vehicle closer to you. The vehicle will be seen in both mirrors. As it starts to pass on the driver's side there will be full vision in both mirrors until it appears in plain sight through the side window.

It is a similar story when a vehicle approaches from the passenger side except as it starts to overtake it enters a blind spot. This is when you need your co-pilot to be awake so that advice can be given for the exact positioning of the car. Another way around this would be to fit a wide angle lens known as a Fresnel lens.

Setting the up mirrors is quite easy as they are electronic. The flat mirror, which is the top one, shows the true size and distance; the bottom mirror which is the convex mirror is used constantly and makes objects look closer than they are.

As you look out of the flat mirror you set it up to see about one inch of the side of the coach; the rest will show you straight back, the purpose being to show you what's approaching from a distance of up to a mile. The convex mirror, also the mirror you use every time you make a turn, needs to be adjusted so one quarter of the mirror looks downwards at the coach side and the rest will look out further to the side to show what is coming alongside from around a quarter of a mile away.

The Rear View Monitor

This is an electronic rear-view camera which shows what is immediately behind the coach. The picture is shown on a monitor on the dashboard. The camera should be set so that the coach is only seen in the lower quarter to half inch of the monitor.

To know how far something is away we needed to use some narrow sticky tape. First measure three metres away from the back bumper of the coach and place an object, cone or bottle, on the ground. Go inside and mark the monitor with the pin stripe tape at the point where the bottle or cone appears on the monitor. This line now represents three metres and if something drives beyond that line it is within three metres of the coach. The amount of distance the monitor shows varies according to the make and model of the coach. To find the distance, drive your car to within metres of the rear bumper of the coach, slowly drive forward until the car reaches the top of the monitor, then measure the distance between coach and car. That measurement is the distance the rear-view monitor is showing you. Of course, when we began towing our jeep all this became irrelevant; nevertheless, the camera and monitor were very useful in making sure the jeep was still attached to the coach. Yes! It has happened.

Next was Negotiating Curves.

This is very different from driving a car. One reason is because the driver sits up very high in the coach, which results in a front end blind spot. The driver has to compensate. This is where Barney's "Dot System" comes into play.

Measure sixteen feet from the front bumper of the coach in front of the steering wheel and place a water bottle or cone on the ground to mark the spot. Now sit in the driver's seat, notice where the bottle or cone is and put a sticky dot on the wind screen exactly where you see the bottle or cone. Once the dot is in place you know where sixteen feet is in front of you, right at that dot. When driving and approaching a left hand corner, slowly drive forward until the dot reaches the far edge of the road in front, then, and only then, make your turn. Although this feels uncomfortable at first it really does work. This method is different when turning right. In this case slowly approach the bend, move forward until the dot is in the middle of the oncoming lane before making the turn. This must be done very slowly.

Next we learnt How to Turn.

This is how to turn onto highways, not car parks. This is when you need to know Bay Star's degree of wheel cut. Wheel cut is the measurement in degrees of how far the wheels turn from the straight position all the way to the right or left. It turned out our wheel cut was fifty degrees, I needed to know this because it helps give the reference point for making a turn. I learnt that my reference point for The Bay Star was my hips. This means that before making a turn, assess where you are going and also what you don't want to hit such as a kerb, sign post or fire hydrant. Then drive slowly forward until your reference point, in my case my hips, are just past the kerb, or other obstacle and very slowly make the turn. This system works for both right and left turns, although left turns are much easier.

Barney then gave us some good advice. Do not panic if things go wrong. "If you make too wide a right hand turn and cut off the oncoming traffic, wait patiently for the traffic lights to change and let the cars in the oncoming lane go round you. You won't be voted best coach driver of the year, but you probably will never meet these people again in your lifetime." Another do not panic piece of advice he gave us was what to do if we drove past a turn off we should have taken. There's no reversing with these giants in many places, and absolutely none if towing a jeep. Don't panic, he said. Just make a left turn, then go left, left, and left again and you will be back in the correct road to make the turn off you should have taken in the first place. Failing that, he said, find a Walmart and turn round in their car park.

After a coffee break which included doughnuts – what else – we were taught about Reversing into a Campsite . This was clearly a more difficult session and we were grateful for the break.

Reversing can be most intimidating, but Barney once again had a system which works, again using the sticky spot system. A few points to note:

Reversing is the most dangerous manoeuvre you can do in a coach. It is easier if you have a partner to act as a spotter to help you.

The best place for the spotter to stand is at the rear end of the coach on the driver's side. The driver must be able to see the spotter at all times. If the driver cannot see the spotter, the driver must not move the coach until such time as the spotter can be seen.

The spotter must use very clear hand signals to communicate with the driver; there must never be any confusion.

To get started you need to mark the coach. At the side of the coach you need to go to the centre of the back tyre and measure forward eight feet and mark the side of the coach with a sticker or dot. Do the same on the other side of the coach. This is known as the eight foot mark and is used every time the coach is reversed into a siding.

Barney calls his reversing method the three-in-one.

Within your selected parking spot imagine a line about one to one-and-a-half feet away from the edge; this line is where you want the driver's side wheels to end up when parked. Drive over to the left about one to two feet from the edge of the road and drive the coach forward until your hips are in line with the imaginary line. This is position no. 1.

Now the spotter is going to come to the driver's side, stand on this imaginary line about an arm's length from the coach. The driver is now going to drive forward, the spotter will signal to stop the coach when the eight-foot mark is on the imaginary line. The driver cannot see the eight-foot mark which makes the spotter the driver's eyes. This is position 2.

The driver will turn the wheel all the way to the right, once this has been turned to the maximum distance to the right, the driver will slowly drive the coach forward and look into the mirror for the spotter who will remain in the same place as position 2. The driver will continue to drive the coach forward until he can no longer see the spotter's right shoulder in the top mirror. The driver will then stop the coach. This is position three.

The spotter will now back up into position and bring the coach into the campsite. The driver will then turn the wheel all the way to the left, look into the mirror and follow the spotter's signals as the coach is backed into the siding. This is the one of the three-in-one.

The above is for reversing into an opening on the driver's side. It's important to note that it is so much easier to back into a campsite from the driver's side.

It is also much easier to select a "drive through" parking spot, no reversing, although these always seemed to fill up first. There's a surprise!

This was the end of the theory part of the course; I felt quite mentally exhausted. This was when Barney gave us some more advice.

This is related to filling the fuel tank. To fill a fuel tank of an RV can take a good twenty minutes; I know with us it was a great time to stretch our legs and have a bit of a break. His advice was simply, make sure before you leave, to take all belongings with you. He then related this story to us.

It was a Friday night and the couple had planned to get away for the weekend. Having packed all items the night before, the couple decided to meet up immediately after work and head on out to an RV Rally. As they set off the wife had a headache and decided to lie down on the bed in the back of the coach as the husband did the driving. The husband drove on as usual and later stopped to fill up the tank. The wife awoke, got up, took the opportunity to go and buy some last minute items from the shop; she was about ten minutes. The husband finished filling the tank and went to pay, after which he drove on, no problem. He was about one hundred and seventy five miles down the road, some three hours later, when he was pulled over by State Troopers. They asked him if they could speak with his wife. The husband, somewhat concerned, wondered why State Troopers would want anything to do with his wife, what had she done? He explained his wife was unwell but went to the bedroom to get her. She was nowhere to be found. The Troopers knew why, because the wife had called them to ask them to stop her husband who had unwittingly abandoned her at the gas station. The Troopers found the situation very amusing.

You see, most of the exit doors are on the right, most of the gas fillers are on the left, and because of the height of the coach it is impossible to see from the pumps anyone exiting the coach.

Always follow Barney's advice. Make sure you take all your belongings with you.

That evening over dinner I could think of nothing else but driving a forty five footer the following day, I passed all my newly acquired knowledge onto the three boys including the amusing story of the wife who got left behind.

The next afternoon I arrived early and took one look at this rather intimidating monster and began to panic. It was a huge diesel pusher, and extremely posh. I hoped nerves were not going to get the better of me. There were just four couples who turned up, plus me. Barney made each of us laboriously put all the dots, stickers and line tape on the correct places after having carefully measured for each purpose. We took our turns driving around the massive car park, turning right and left covering all the moves possible. I was very surprised as this was nowhere near as difficult as imagined, providing you kept to the rules and followed the instructions. The most nerve-racking thing was having the other students sitting behind watching your every move. After about five minutes I quite forgot I was driving a forty-five foot coach and it felt quite comfortable. The only difficulty I had to deal with, the obvious one that I had quite forgotten, was that I was driving on the "wrong" side of the road; I kept that quiet. My first attempt at parking into the slot was not too good, but not a complete disaster, my second hit the spot and got a well done from Barney. I was also very good as a spotter, so I was beginning to wonder if I should give up my day job. Barney also taught us how a co-pilot should take over from the driver in an emergency such as a heart attack. I excelled at this. I was up for anything with a bit of drama.

I mentioned driving on the "wrong" side of the road. Americans consider that we Brits drive on the "wrong" side of the road.

Just to set the record straight. Driving on the left is the "correct" side of the road. When people rode horses they always rode on the left, in order to give their right arm free space to use their sword or lance, and in later days their gun. Most people are right-handed.

When there is any physical threat it is a fact that most

humans will duck or dive to the left. Thus, a British driver will swerve left into the hedge. An American driver will swerve left into the oncoming traffic. What more can I say?

Except, could I be forgiven for saying that I'm right to write that right is wrong. BUT, if I am right, how come approximately two thirds of the world's population drive on the wrong side – or right side?!

I was very disappointed when the instruction came to an end and I was tempted to sign up for another day, but alas I didn't. We said our goodbyes and thanked Barney for the invaluable instruction and went on our way.

Little did I know that sadly this was the last time I would drive an RV, or at least on this trip.

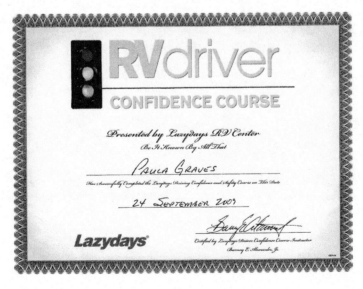

Mum's driving certificate

September 25 2009
I am writing from tapa
(Florida) we have Ruchased
a 40 foot coach (Bighw)
and quite an old Jeep.
weve been here for two weeks,
Josh and me have taken
to our bunk beds like Eglish
to fish and chips.
Mum and dad are talking
the lazdays comfed course
and mums got a certificate
I am very proud of mum,

Jakes diary

NEW ORLEANS

When I asked the boys what recollections they had about New Orleans, Josh immediately referred to the jazz music. Jake also had an instant reply: Bourbon Street with Jazz players. As for Keith and myself, we will always remember the uneasy feeling we experienced when we drove for the first time down Basin St, taking in the police cars, blue lights flashing, the men, women and children at the side of the road, on the pavements and porches, unsure what their faces were saying to us. The Americans refer to this area as low income, but the words rundown, neglect, poverty and even dangerous would be a more suitable description. A few minutes later, having missed our turning, unable to reverse, we tried out for the first time the left, left, left and left sequence that Barney had drummed into us. We drove back along the same street. This time we read the depressing truth of the sheer hopelessness that hurricane Katrina had left these people. Appalled that after nearly four years the neighbourhood hadn't been "fixed". Why? Sadly for me the Basin Street Blues has taken on a different interpretation.

Let's go back to yesterday and the start of our journey to this amazing city.

Last night, being our first on the road, was exciting and yet uneventful. We arrived at The Big Oak Rally Park in Tallahassee, a very pretty site with all the amenities required for one night. We successfully plugged in all our attachments and put out the slides. At first the boys were a bit nervous about using the shower facilities at the campsite but soon got into the system. The routine of Jake with Dad and Josh with Mum seemed to work OK. By law boys over the age of ten were not allowed in the ladies' rooms. We were all looking forward to tomorrow, a big day on the road to New Orleans.

It was very clear when we left Tallahassee that our routines regarding the arrival and leaving the campsites were most definitely becoming more slick and professional. I was not only directing the coach out of the parking space, with clear and precise hand signals, but was also responsibly making sure all outdoor items came with us. Steps, umbrellas, buckets etc. Only once did we leave a pair of Keith's shoes behind. As soon as I boarded the coach my next routine would start. I became a stewardess, making sure all seatbelts were on, overhead lockers were secure, and all items were tucked safely somewhere. During the journey I also provided the drinks and snacks. Keith too had his duties before we left the sites. Unplugging the sewage system (someone's got to do it!), ensuring the slides were in and secure, and of course general engine checks. The task of securing the jeep to the coach was a joint effort. I was also light monitor, ensuring brake lights, indicator lights and driving lights were all functioning properly on both the coach and the jeep, and signalling the results to Keith in the driving seat. The boys were responsible for making their own beds and tidying all their clothes, toys and books. There was no room for untidiness on our coach. Surprisingly enough this was never a problem.

We tried where possible never to be more than five hours between campsites, preferably three. The exception to this was the trip to New Orleans. This took close to six hours, driving around six hundred kilometres. With all this travelling time, it seemed sensible to do some home schooling. We often studied the route we were taking, the different states we were driving through, and basic background to the place we were heading for. On this journey we spoke of Jazz, Creole Food, and the American Civil Rights movement. Jake was also very interested in politics, especially as Obama was a relatively "new" first black president, and he quickly latched onto the Rosa Parks story with real enthusiasm. Josh much preferred the music stories which introduced Louis Armstrong. As for me, I was getting more excited as we came closer to this amazing town.

When not home schooling, my position in the coach is

of course next to the driver. This is the very best seat in the house, the view is superb, and the comfort level is high. The chair has all the attributes of a comfy armchair. It can recline almost flat and comes with a footrest. The soft armrests and the cup holders are, as you would expect, in the perfect place.

As we approached the city the road changed drastically becoming narrower and narrower, the broad American highway no longer with us, being replaced with "French style" country roads. We went sailing past our campsite as we got closer to the French quarter. Trying to find a way back, bearing in mind you can't reverse when towing, we drove along Basin St three times before we finally arrived at the entrance to the campsite. Keith did exceptionally well as it was indeed a bit nerve-racking negotiating these very narrow roads with a thirty-four foot vehicle towing a Jeep. Barney's left, left, left and left system worked a treat. Boy did we need it. A hero most certainly.

The campsite was situated between Basin St and the French Quarter. We were greeted by a security guard who assured us the site itself was very safe. As long as we didn't venture through Basin St, particularly at night, no harm would come to us. The site itself was very comfortable, housing a pool and BBQ area. All the amenities were spotless and very tasteful.

I have to say our stay in New Orleans was far too short – hindsight is a wonderful thing – but we squeezed in as much as we could. As we entered the French quarter the feeling of 'we have arrived' hit us all. Jazz musicians on every street corner, Voodoo threatening scarily from shop windows, Café du Monde, Paddle steamers, Filigumbo, Crawfish Pie, Jambalaya and so much more.

The French Quarter itself is the small, but most famous part of New Orleans. The area starts along the Mississippi river from Canal St to Esplanade Avenue and inland to N. Rampart St. The total area is roughly 78 "square blocks". Most of the buildings in this area date back to the early 1800s and are protected by law. which means that they cannot be demolished.

Voodoo is so much a part of New Orleans, creating part of this rich culture. Just watching tourists buy the voodoo dolls, charms and amulets, each promising to bring protection from anything that is at all menacing, is somewhat addictive to say the least. It didn't take us long before we were all rummaging through the heaps of souvenirs in search of that one all-important protector. I say all, not too sure if Keith shared our enthusiasm, but he played along all the same. Maybe he was just a bit frightened! There is of course a serious side to voodoo that in my opinion demands a certain respect. A side that is dark and untouchable to a mere onlooker. The boys were very excited at the thought of such untouchable evil, a little worrying for a parent you might think, but seeing them moonwalking from shop to shop put our minds at rest, and to our relief the excitement was more for Michael Jackson and his rereleased Thriller album. A superb combination with

New Orleans, don't you think?

Jazz and blues music, love it or hate it, has to be the heart of New Orleans. Know it as Marching band music, Dixie land, New Orleans Blues, Ragtime, or simply New Orleans music. Buddy Bolden, cornet player, was probably the first Jazz musician to be respected. Jazz became very popular from 1890, and later gained momentum with the New Orleans born Louis Armstrong in the 1920s. We loved it, we couldn't get enough of it! The Jazz bands playing on every street corner were well organized, each having their individual allocated time slots. Each band offering a different style to the previous one. It is very difficult, nigh on impossible, to just listen to this music without dancing, hence the many groups of street dancers, mostly tourists, who took to the streets dancing in any style. It all worked. The boys were hooked. A real carnival atmosphere that seemed a normal part of New Orleans daily life.

Walking through the French Quarter you eventually arrive at the docks where the Steam Ships can be admired. Basically, a paddle steamer is a steamship or riverboat powered by a steam engine which drives paddle wheels, one on either side, or a single one at the back, to propel the craft through water. The one we saw and photographed was called The Natchez. These paddle steamers are truly magnificent, almost elegant, as they take onboard their passengers. The Mississippi river and its paddle steamers were the lifeblood of the South, carrying passengers and cargo throughout the area. They were also dens of iniquity, hosting gambling and "Ladies of the Night".

It was somewhere close to this area that we stopped in the famous Café Du Monde. Nowadays there is more than one, but the original first opened in 1862 in the French market serving just dark roasted coffee and chicory, black or au lait, chocolate milk, fresh orange juice and Beignets. Originally these Beignets were fritters that were sometimes filled with fruit. Today's adaptation is a square piece of dough, fried, and covered with icing sugar. Enjoyed, I must say, by us all. They were delicious!

As a family we have always enjoyed food! Living in Asia meant that we were spoilt with so much choice that it became the norm to be able to choose between Chinese, Korean, Malaysian, Thai, or Vietnamese, and of course Western, on a daily basis. When we arrived in America the everyday choices were very different. At first the boys relished the fact that fries were available with every meal, but after a time they began to long for a more varied diet. This was easy to rectify when cooking from the coach, but we found some of the more family-oriented restaurants more limited in their choice. This all changed in New Orleans and we were introduced to yet another cuisine. To make it simple I will call it New Orleans cuisine.

This to us was new and exciting, we couldn't wait to try. The Carpenters song kept playing through my mind and we just had to try Jambalaya, Crawfish pie and Filigumbo.

But what kind of food is it? First of all the basics of Creole and Cajun need to be explained. Creole, its style originating in Louisiana, it really mixes European, French, Italian, Portuguese and Spanish, with American and African cuisines. Put these influences together with the Southern style and you have Creole. Creole has been described as City food. Cajun, on the other hand, is similar to Creole but is more rustic, robust and spicy. Cajun used to be referred to as peasant food as it was developed by the Acadians learning to live in the Louisiana swamps. Nowadays both cuisines have developed and are at times difficult to differentiate.

With this is mind, we thoroughly enjoyed our time sampling New Orleans cuisine. Jambalaya: Essentially a rice dish with seafood, chicken and andouille (smoked sausage), stock and vegetables. Saffron is often used with other spices. Gumbo: Made from a thick strongly flavoured stock with seafood, meat and vegetables, resembling a hearty stew. Crawfish pie: A pie packed with crayfish and vegetables, delicious and very filling.

New Orleans is also famous for its cocktails. A Sazerac, from Rye Whisky and bitters, went down a treat.

All good things come to an end and it was now time to move on, taking with us rich memories that this city was kind enough to give.

The French Quarter

Natchez

HOUSTON, TEXAS

It was a battle I was losing. I was now in little doubt that my chances of sharing at least some of the coach driving were disappearing fast. Keith, who has always been very complimentary about my driving (assuming we ignore my parking abilities), and who has always been complimentary towards women drivers in general, has now given me an ultimatum. If I drive he will have no choice but to hibernate for the duration of the journey in our bedroom at the back of the coach with the door closed and television on loud, until the ordeal is over. He felt unable to be co-pilot. The co-pilot's job is to help support the driver whenever possible. Let's not forget that driving on a different side of the road on strange roads and in traffic which one has never experienced before requires the full concentration of the driver. Driving a huge new vehicle towing a Jeep without the backing of one's fellow companion does little to strengthen confidence, let alone help with the safety issues.

Now before we all boo and throw rotten eggs in Keith's direction, let's try to be fair; he's my husband, I love him. There are quite a few men and women out there, who once they get behind the wheel of a car for some reason undergo a complete personality change. Many become irrational, most become impatient, some pay too much attention to others' mistakes hence road rage, some become hungry and are constantly trying to find food hidden in the depths of a lost bag underneath the passenger seat, some are continuously fiddling with the electronics, some talk on the phone and text, and let's not forget the daydreamers who never seem to notice when the lights change. Not forgetting the ladies who just occasionally use the mirrors for grooming purposes.

The Keiths of this world are in actual fact very good drivers. There are a few. However, some of these drivers, bless them, have to be in control of the vehicle whether they are driving or not, thus making them impossible passengers. So what was I to do? I was pretty sure he wouldn't agree to go on a "How to Stop Being a Control Nut Passenger" course. I have to say he hates being driven by anybody including Taxi and Bus drivers. I'm often surprised he allows pilots to fly any plane he is on. This, of course, resulted in me operating from the co-pilot's seat.

So exactly how bad was this for me? I really did want to help with the driving and from a safety aspect this should have been mandatory – after all, Keith could meet with an accident, have a heart attack or catch that particular type of flu, in which case I would have to step in at a moment's notice. I had passed my driving course, therefore it made sense to get in some practice. I would have been happy just driving on the highways now and again with the odd bit of parking thrown in, because I so wanted to test again Barney's sticker system. Nevertheless, I was really enjoying the on the road groundwork chats with the boys and was also beginning to really appreciate being a passenger. My spot in the coach without a doubt was certainly comparable to any first-class seat in long haul air travel. So, life wasn't so bad, and as I really view Keith's driving attitude as a freak mental disorder, I just moved on.

Our next stop was Houston in Texas, approximately three hundred and fifty miles, mostly along the I10 west, around a five-hour trip. We were fascinated as we watched the luscious, dank, alligator infested swamps of Louisiana gradually change into the seemingly endless flat and boring Texas oil fields. We took the opportunity to find out a bit about Texas. It was obvious that oil was an important part of the Texan/American economy with so many oil fields and so much equipment, land rigs, drilling rigs, oil pumps all constantly moving. These pumps are nicknamed Nodding Donkeys because they resemble donkeys grazing as they move up and down almost hypnotically. In fact, Texas is the largest oil and natural gas daily provider in the US with over one hundred and fifty thousand active oil wells and nearly sixty-seven thousand active gas wells, so we were definitely passing through Ewing country.

Texas is nicknamed the Lone Star State and has always been extremely independent. In fact, Texas was once a country in its own right, its flag having only one star on it to symbolise Texas alone, hence the nickname. During the Texan Revolution in the 1830s Texas won its independence from Mexico. One hundred and eighty-seven volunteers defended a fort known as the Alamo for thirteen days. All the Texans at the fort were killed, but it was Sam Houston who went on to win the revolution by inspiring his soldiers with the battle cry "Remember the Alamo". It has been part of the Statehood since 1845. It is the second most populous of the fifty states with 26.54 million people and it is the second largest, covering 268, 820 sq. miles, almost twice the size of the United Kingdom. The capital city is Austin.

We were on the lookout for the Bluebonnet which is the state flower and the mocking bird being the state bird.

After a lunch stop the boys were relaxing back in their seats to enjoy the rest of the journey into Houston. We talked a little about NASA and our forthcoming visit, which led to one of the boys asking about David Bowie's song Space Odyssey, and we realised we didn't know all the words to the song, and that the words we did know didn't really make any sense. We soon found them, and began singing; it certainly helped pass the time, so in just a few hours we had swapped The Carpenter's Jambalaya (on the Bayou) to David Bowie. We all enjoyed the change. At least for a few miles.

We were about ten miles away from our RV site, or our "final destination" as Flossie would say. When Keith needed some help with the navigation and he asked me, this was when I knew he was getting tired of the singing .No one, at least anyone who knows me, would ever ask me the directions to anywhere. I can be relied on to turn the wrong way out of a lift on any floor in any hotel in the world, and can guarantee the whole of my family will automatically turn the opposite way. I now had to, alone, navigate around a system that makes Spaghetti Junction resemble a country road in the Outer Hebrides. Nevertheless, Keith asked me. Being a down to earth, common sense, think on your feet individual, I found a way. Flossie needed an interpreter, and I was the one for the job. I just stepped up to the challenge.

Just to explain, Flossie is our All-American Sat Nav, so the conversation went as follows:

Flossie: Come off the turnpike at the next exit

Paula: Take the next exit off the highway.

Keith: That doesn't look right, it's too soon to come off. I'll take the one after.

Keith: Where to now?

Flossie: [Taking her time to recalculate] Go straight at the next four way and take a right at the intersection.

Paula: Go straight at the next crossroads and turn right at the junction.

Keith: But that's the wrong direction.

Keith indeed went straight at the crossroads but missed the right turn.

This performance, and what a performance it was, went on for another forty-five minutes at least. It was then that we agreed to phone the campsite and try to get directions. As they were expecting us, they were anticipating a call, and they had seen our coach sail by a few times on the highway. We had been clocked. It was agreed that we would be talked in by a very helpful, polite Texan. We had forgotten to turn Flossie off, but it was most interesting. Flossie was mimicking our guide word for word. Funny that.

The Advanced RV Centre site was great, spacious, spotlessly clean, swimming pool, private bathrooms, restaurant, camping shop and more. More importantly the staff were most helpful. It was clear we were going to have an enjoyable stay.

The next day was about buying the all-important provisions and relaxing within the campsite, so we set off to find the nearest supermarket. This wasn't too far away but we had to negotiate the complex road system again and ran into the same problem. This time Keith trusted Flossie (and the interpreter) and arrived back home without too many hiccups. Just one thing to note here, the Texans we had met so far really stood out as original, courteous and very helpful. Our only reservation was the boys seemed to have picked up their next Americanism. "Well pat ma heinie and smell ma pitts." This has many uses. Imagine you come over the crest of a hill and a stunning view unfolds. What else is to be said but: "Well pat ma heinie and smell ma pitts"? Similarly if they are asked to wash the dishes in the middle of a Disney film:. "Aw shucks well pat..." I'm sure you get the drift!!

We spent the afternoon talking about NASA in preparation for the next day's trip. It was clear that both Keith and I were getting excited about this trip and we were animated to say the least. NASA, National Aeronautics and Space Administration, is an agency of the United States Government and it is responsible for the nation's civilian Space Program. Established in 1958 by President Dwight Eisenhower, the emphasis being on a neutral American body that would encourage peaceful applications in Space Science.

Having remembered some of the Apollo missions from our childhood, we were looking forward to sharing all our memories with the boys. The Apollo program included both manned and unmanned space missions, flown by NASA between 1961 and 1975. The first manned Apollo mission was Apollo 7. The most famous of all was the Apollo 11 Lunar module; it was July 20th 1969 that this space craft landed in the Sea of Tranquillity. Astronauts Neil Armstrong and Buzz Aldrin performed a single EVA in the vicinity of the Lunar

Module on July 21st 1969, Armstrong, meeting Kennedy's challenge, was the first to step on the lunar surface with the words "One small step for [a] man, one giant leap for mankind".

By the way EVA means Extra-vehicular Activity, which is an activity done by an Astronaut or Cosmonaut outside a space craft beyond the earth's atmosphere. The term most commonly applies to a spacewalk made outside a craft orbiting the earth.

Apollo 17 was the final Lunar mission; Schmitt a geologist was the first professional scientist to go on a NASA mission.

I recall being on holiday in the Isle of Wight with Mum and Dad when Apollo 11 returned to Earth; it was a nail biting time as we all crowded around a television set in the lounge of our hotel waiting for the astronauts to re-enter the Earth's atmosphere. When they did, I had to cover my ears because the sheer volume of the shrieks and cheers from everyone was just too much. I also remember the tears and hugs of relief.

Keith's memories were of the moon landings themselves with Neil Armstrong and Buzz Aldrin walking and jumping on the moon's surface with all their equipment including the US flag, absolutely amazed that the conversation between the astronauts themselves could be heard.

By now we had worked ourselves into a state of feverish excitement; we couldn't wait for the next day.

The Johnson Space Center was easy to find, 1601, Parkway,

Houston. Texas, 77058. A very people friendly place to visit for all ages. The boys soon found the Kids Space place, which is for any child who dares to dream of becoming an astronaut. They disappeared for about half an hour leaving us parents time to try to organise the day's events.

Next we experienced one of the theatres. I think it was called The Blast Off theatre, or it should have been as we underwent a launching into Space just like a real astronaut. After this I really understand the meaning of the Wow factor.

The Starships Gallery was next on the agenda where we could see exhibits of the US Space program including the vault containing moon rocks. To actually be standing a few feet away from them and also to be next to one of the actual Apollo capsules was really something else.

The Tram Tour for me was superb as it took us to some of the many current working areas as well as to some of the more historic places like the Apollo Mission Control centre. To walk into the mission control centre, the actual centre where all the communications took place from the Earth to the Moon brought back to mind all the black and white childhood memories of the numerous news reports including all the countdowns to the Apollo missions. Exciting times.

Continuing on with the tram tour we visited the new Mission Control centre. As tourists we were only allowed into the certain allotted places at the rear of the large room. Here we learnt a lot of the real background to the Johnson

Space Center. Originally known as the Manned Spacecraft Centre, after years of development it changed its name in honour of the 36th US President, Lyndon Baines Johnson, a native of Texas. Officially it is the National Aeronautics and Space Administration centre for human spaceflight training, research and flight control. The centre itself is large and constructed on 1,620 acres; it houses a complex of over one hundred buildings. Its responsibilities include Astronaut training of both US and International partners. Globally it is fondly known as Mission Control; however, no spacecraft has ever been launched from here. In the USA space rockets take off from Florida.

Mission Control coordinates and monitors all human space flights for the US. The Centre directs and oversees all Space Shuttle missions and happenings involving the International Space Station, no matter which country has launched them. From the instant a manned space craft leaves its launch tower until the time it arrives back on Earth, it is in the hands of Mission Control. There are several flight control rooms from which the flight controllers monitor and organise the space flights. When a mission is underway, the control rooms are manned around the clock in three shifts. It was interesting to be told that the Control Director, when in charge of a Space Mission, has more power over the mission than the President of the United States.

We were lucky that day, as the controllers were in

communication with the astronauts at the ISS. The International Space Station is in low orbit, and at certain times can be seen by the naked eye from Earth.

The training for the Astronauts as one would expect is very extensive and indeed intensive. An example is the training for the moonwalks and weightlessness. The Neutral Buoyancy Lab provides a controlled neutral buoyancy environment. This is a large pool containing 6.2 million US gallons of water (about 5 million UK gallons); it only takes 660,500 gallons to fill an Olympic swimming pool. In this water the astronauts practise their EVA tasks simulating zero gravity conditions, helping them become familiar with all the crew activities and learning about the dynamics of body motion.

We all learnt a lot the day of our visit, and realised what an enormous achievement it was back in the sixties to successfully land humans on the Moon. There was talk of man landing on Mars the red planet by 2020, but as always overcoming budget obstacles is never easy which has resulted in a different time and many of the technologies are not yet in place. Charles Bolden, who is the current administrator of NASA, has now unveiled plans and targets to achieve this by 2035.

Over dinner that evening discussing NASA and Space travel in general I couldn't help but notice the enthusiasm and sheer stimulation that was being produced around the table came more from the adults than the children. It was obvious that the boys had a great day, but they didn't seem to share the same elation as us adults. Then it dawned on us that Star Wars, a firm favourite, is far more sophisticated and advanced than mere moon landings by NASA – could this be the reason? Could virtual ever lead the way to reality? Now there's a thought.

As soon as we passed a road sign to Historic Route 66, Keith burst into song. We debated who the original singer was – I for one only really remembered the Rolling Stones version, Keith recalled the Chuck Berry hit, but it was actually written in 1946 by Bobby Troup, native of Pennsylvania and made famous by Nat King Cole as the King Cole Trio. He was then 27. The song came to symbolise freedom and adventure, sentiments we were beginning to realise through our various travels. John Steinbeck's Pulitzer Prize winning novel "The Grapes of Wrath" devoted a whole chapter to Route 66, and this was where the nickname The Mother Road was born, a nickname that stuck. Steinbeck dealt with The Great Depression and migrants who fled drought and poverty in Oklahoma, Texas and neighbouring States as they travelled west along Route 66 in search of employment.

Elk City, Oklahoma, found in Beckham County, is around 500 miles away from Houston and we decided to take it easy, stopping for a night at Hidden Lake RV Park. The whole journey itself took us via I-45N, US-287N, and was an ideal time to do some investigative work with the boys on Oklahoma and Route 66.

We learnt the statehood was granted in 1907, the capital is Oklahoma City, nicknamed The Sooner State. The State flower is the mistletoe and State bird the Scissor tailed flycatcher. Oklahoma boasts that there is so much oil underground that many people got rich by discovering oil in their own back yards; this is often referred to as Oklahoma's "Black Gold".

In 1889, the United States opened the Oklahoma Territory for settlement. A gun was fired to start the land rush, but some eager, or greedy settlers jumped the gun to claim the best of the land early. The Sooner State gets its name from these pioneers who got there "sooner".

The next fact the boys seemed fascinated by was that most of the Indian tribes who now live in Oklahoma were forced to walk there by the United States government during the 1800s. This journey became known as the Trail of Tears because so many died on the way. This captured Jake's interest and he decided his next project was going to be about the various Indian Tribes of America. As Oklahoma is home to at least 55 Indian Nations alone, we agreed that he would certainly have a busy time ahead. It's fascinating that each of these Indian Nations not only has its own language or dialect, but each tribe controls its own government schools and land, and in addition the Indian Nations have the right to open gambling casinos on reservation land whereas in the rest of the USA this is strictly controlled. The name Oklahoma comes from two Choctaw Indian words humma and Okla, meaning red people. The next day we planned to visit the museum on Route 66, another cue for the song but this time the two boys sang as well. I would have joined them, but was busy navigating and my aptitude for that and for singing are equally well known.

The National Route 66 museum consists not only of the Transport museum but incorporates Old Town Farm Ranch museum and a Blacksmiths museum. We started at the Transport museum, which was full of memorabilia from the Route 66 heyday as well as displays of antique cars and many interactive hands-on displays. The boys got a feel of what it was like to drive down Route 66 in a pink 1950s' Cadillac. It also focussed on the people who travelled, worked and lived on the route, and the way many towns and businesses were developed. Established in 1926, the route was known by other names such as The Will Rogers Highway, The Main Street of America and the Mother Road. It ran from Chicago, Illinois through Missouri, Kansas, Oklahoma, Texas, New Mexico, Arizona to Santa Monica, California where it ends. It covers a total of 2448 miles

State	Miles	KM
Illinois	301	484
Missouri	317	510
Kansas	13	21
Oklahoma	432	695
Texas	186	299
New Mexico	487	784
Arizona	401	645
California	314	505

It was President Eisenhower who signed a Federal Aid Highway act which established America's 47,800 mile Interstate Highway System which eventually led to Route 66 becoming obsolete. Its revival to The Historic Route 66 happened in the late 1980s. It was later in our American journey we discovered a motorist's green book written by Victor H Green who was a postal worker. This was a travel guide for African-Americans featuring friendly places to stay, eat and shop en route as many motels and restaurants on Route 66 were banned to black people. The book was first published in 1936 and the Green Book series continued to be updated and published until 1966.

Next we entered the Old Town Museum, which was a replica of small town life as it would have been back in the 1930s, comprising a Doctor's house, schoolhouse and chapel and a Victorian-style house. We walked through the town and entered the Victorian house, the downstairs of which gave us a glimpse into early pioneer life; we noted the Stars and Stripes room and a Native American Gallery. It was the upper floor that was more interesting to the boys as it was devoted to the early cowboy and rodeo way of life.

We quickly walked through the Farm and Ranch museum and then through to the Blacksmiths museum and by this time we were hungry and decided to call it a day. Tomorrow we were moving on and we needed to discuss our next destinations. We took with us some lovely memories of Oklahoma and Route 66.

THE PAINTED DESERT

The Internet was started in the 1960s by the USA military, but did not come into general commercial use until the 1980s. It is little wonder, therefore, that my generation is so thankful for it. Although we survived quite comfortably through the dark Encyclopaedia Britannica ages using telex and fax to communicate, it is still a novelty to gain access to so much instant information. It certainly made for more lively and relevant on-the-road teaching sessions, and enhanced our humanities and geography lessons. Whilst we were all looking forward to moving on to the Painted Desert, Arizona, we had very little idea what to expect, and it was Wikipedia which provided the most insight, preparing us step-by-step for the experience that was to come. But before this we had to drive from Santa Rosa, New Mexico, where we had spent the night, to Holbrooke in Arizona where we had planned a three night stop.

We were going to be travelling for approximately three hundred and fifty miles through New Mexico to Arizona providing plenty of time to help the boys discover more about New Mexico State, as it was relatively unknown to us. Americans have nicknames for all their states and we liked the one for New Mexico: "The Land of Enchantment". It has been part of the Statehood since 1912. The State flower is the Yucca and the State bird the Roadrunner which is such a funny looking specimen with its long neck, quick movements and funny run and walk, totally true to the roadrunner in cartoons. This delighted the boys and led to a most infectious fit of the giggles.

Spanish explorers named the area New Mexico when they first came north from Mexico way back in 1540, and we learned that in some parts of the State you can see pottery from the Anasazi Indians dating back more than two thousand years. We drove past Albuquerque, known for its annual air balloon festival, which sadly we had missed by two days. We were travelling through Indian Reservation country. We noticed the scenery was changing, becoming dryer and dustier, and the buildings were very different to the ones we had seen so far on our travels in America, or indeed anywhere. They are known as adobe houses. These houses are made from adobe bricks or blocks of clay and straw, which have been dried in the sun. People who live in the desert have been building this type of dwelling for hundreds of years simply because they stay cool in the desert heat, and wood is not readily available. We loved these houses as they gave a very unique Indian, Spanish texture which conjured up images of old Wild West John Wayne films.

After a lunch break, we continued on the road, and returned to our studies with a story about the traditional New Mexican weavers. This community arrived in 1540 with the Coronado expedition, who brought with them over 5,000 Churro Sheep which soon became established flocks and a valued food source. Wool was produced and blankets manufactured, initially in the homes to keep the cold desert mountain nights at bay. A great demand from surrounding trading partners led an industry to develop, employing sheep herders, spinners and weavers. The Rio Grande blanket was born, which encompassed the entire weaving tradition of Hispanic New Mexico. Another famous woven wool item was the Saltillo Serape. The silhouette of this serape is often in fashion today, albeit with a change to the fabric and specification. Today there are many families still carrying on the tradition of the weavers, some small cottage industries, some much larger.

It was late afternoon when we arrived at the campsite in Holbrooke, Arizona. The boys couldn't wait to run around and explore. They soon discovered play areas, cowpoke cookouts, and two new friends, Drew and Will. They were happy! The site was chosen for its easy access to the I-40, which leads to the Painted Desert, Petrified Forest National Park, where we were looking forward to seeing the fossilized logs from pre-dinosaur days. This area is well known for Route 66 memorabilia which we thought worth a visit, along with the Hubbell Trading post on the Navajo Reservation north of the town. This place was going to be interesting and fun.

The next morning we had a delightful breakfast cooked for us by the campsite chef consisting of pancakes with syrup, eggs and bacon. This incidentally sewed a seed in Jake's entrepreneur mind, more of which later. We then headed for The Painted Desert. Not even Wikipedia had prepared us for the sight before us. We all took a few steps back as if viewing a masterpiece, eyeing up each part of the landscape, admiring such perfection, a true wilderness of colour. The morning shades on this day were showing us pigments of the pastel spectrum almost greyed off. There were faint outlines surrounding the various rock shapes, almost giving the impression of a huge paint by numbers canvas.

We were in the North East of Arizona. The desert begins about thirty-five miles north of Cameron near the south eastern rim of the Grand Canyon and runs south east, ending just beyond the Petrified Forest. All this area comes under the Petrified Forest National Park. We hiked around the park's wilderness area, taking in the Painted Desert Inn, which at first glance appears a little run down because it is built of old rubble and stone to make it look hundreds of years old. It was actually built between 1937 and 1940 on the site of an older lodge called the Stone Tree House. It has a café, shop, museum, the National Park Ranger's office and seven letting bedrooms. The dusty cactus strewn terrace has stunning views of the desert. We were in awe of such a colourful backdrop which encompasses over ninety-three thousand acres stretching over one hundred and sixty miles. Much of this region is only accessible by foot or on unpaved roads, although major highways do cut across it. The towns Cameron and Tuba City, two major settlements, are both within the Navajo Nation. A permit is required for all back-road travel in the Navajo Nation.

As we continued our walk we learnt more about the geology of the area. The desert itself comprises layers of easily erodible siltstone, mudstone and shale from the Triassic Chinie Formation. These fine-grained rock layers contain abundant iron, manganese compounds which provide pigments for the various spectacular rock and soil colours of the region. Thin resistant lacustrine limestone layers and volcanic flows cap the mesas. Numerous layers of silicic volcanic ash occur in the Chinie and provide the silica for the petrified logs of the area. The erosion of these layers has resulted in the formation of the Badlands topography.

Named the Badlands of Arizona, mainly because of such dry terrain where the softer sedimentary rocks and clay rich soils have been extensively eroded by wind and water, the Badlands exist only in dry regions with nil vegetation. We walked a couple of miles into another area of the Painted

Desert where the colours changed from pastels to almost black, white, and grey tints. It was as if we had entered an old movie set. The scenery became almost alien. The boys loved the idea of walking through such terrain and with their imaginations on high alert they couldn't wait to explore. After only another five minutes of slow walking we found ourselves in a maze of stone shapes and pathways. The air was becoming cooler, and the silence louder. We kept on walking, nobody was uttering a word; we seemed to be taking soft strides so as not to disturb anyone, although it was pretty clear we were alone. A cool breeze came from nowhere and the boys now were staying close to us listening to the wind, the only sound we could hear. At this point I think we were all ready to encounter that primal fear from the depth of our imaginations. It could have been smoke signals from a hostile Indian tribe just over the hills, or a spaceship landing in the next valley and aliens disembarking. Instead, after about an hour, we slowly made our way back to the softer scenery and our comfort zone. The Arizona Badlands. A walk never to be forgotten.

The next day we discovered the Petrified Forest. This is in the southern part of the desert where the remains of a Triassic period coniferous forest fossilized over millions of years. Wind, water and soil erosion continue to change the face of the landscape by shifting sediment and exposing layers of the Chinie formation. An assortment of fossilized prehistoric plants and animals are found in the region as well as dinosaur tracks and the evidence of early human habitation.

We didn't really know what to expect of this forest and were very surprised at the abundance of logs and tree stumps seemingly everywhere. Having picked up a pair of agate bookends many years ago in Lyme Regis, I now realized how precious these are. Millions of years old, giant logs everywhere. We were pleased to see there were rules in place – visitors were only allowed in certain areas and we were not allowed to take anything from the forest away with us. We walked for an hour among these ancient fallen trees and just marvelled at such phenomena. To actually touch something that is over two hundred million years old sent shivers down my spine. Keith shared my sentiment, but the boys had their own agenda and were busy hunting for dinosaur tracks and signs of other such monsters. This game would have lasted for weeks had it not been for their hunger and the need to spend some of their pocket money on pieces of fossilised wood millions of years old.

The next day the boys created some great pieces of art reflecting the Painted Desert, and spent the rest of the day with their friends Drew and Will, recreating and drawing the Painted Desert National Park. Another visit we will always remember.

Petrified wood

The badlands

The Painted Desert

WILLIAMS, ARIZONA

I loved this small town; it was fun, it had punch, and was oozing with heart. As it was a mere two-and-a-half-hour drive from The Painted Desert on Interstate 40 towards Flagstaff, the journey was easy, and everyone was happy and content, always a good sign when moving to a new destination. When I say everyone, I must omit myself as in truth frustration was taking its toll. My computer, which was fast becoming indispensable in its home-schooling role, had completely blacked out. It was dead to the world. Luckily close by Flagstaff had a Best Buy with a large computer service section that was able to help. However, it was a story which panned out over five days. We learned the cost of repair would be $300 plus, and could not be guaranteed for even a month, therefore with little choice we bought a new computer, transferring all info from the old hard drive. On collection of the new and old computers we found that the old computer had mysteriously mended itself to the surprise of the geeks, which meant we now had two working computers. When we checked everything at home, we found the transfer to the new computer was far from complete, so it was back again to the store. Eventually after two more days we were told the new computer had a faulty hard drive, we were entitled to a full refund and they were able to return all info back again from the new to the old computer. Five days and we were back to the beginning again. At last we were ready to go, but what a faff!

The campsite, The Grand Canyon Railway, was part of Camp Club USA, which meant it was up to a very high standard. It didn't disappoint as all the facilities were 5-star. We arrived just after noon and the campsite was almost empty, which surprised me as the booking wasn't easy to secure; however, around four o'clock the big boys in rather large and very expensive RVs began to arrive. Very impressive, especially as we thought naïvely that our 34-footer plus jeep was large and striking to look at. It was like comparing a smart car to a Range Rover. We soon learnt that a Rally was being held for a few days. An RV Rally is a very social event, a time when everyone from anywhere can get together to compare travel experiences and generally catch up. Always there is organised entertainment, dinners, barbecues, RV seminars and general meetings. Being British with two Chinese children, we were always subject matter for the curious, and we were soon welcomed into the party atmosphere.

We discovered the site had a great indoor pool, which we all enjoyed, and afterwards provisions were required. Keith and I went in search of a supermarket; this was surprisingly easy as a familiar Safeway was virtually next-door. This bought back memories of food shopping many years ago in Kensington, London. By American standards Williams is a very small town nestled in the pine country of Arizona in Coconino County, west of Flagstaff. Very attractive to the tourist as you not only can ride the Grand Canyon Railway through areas typical of Arizona, but from its southern terminus it takes tourists all the way to the Grand Canyon village. A great holiday destination with the Bearizona wildlife park on its doorstep offering fishing, hiking, horseback riding and basic camping. Scattered in and around Williams are many motor lodges, small hotels and some historic accommodations, along with numerous restaurants with home cooked American fare.

We were already Route 66 fans, which could be the reason why we loved this town so much, being one of the last towns to be bypassed by Interstate 40 in October 1984. It gave a very good idea of how life must have been on Route 66. There are at least six blocks of restaurants and shops, offering all sorts of memorabilia from tacky to quite stylish. It was on one of these blocks we encountered an antique-style shop with its charming owners who were only too pleased, in their colourful way, to show us around and introduce us to the world of real antiques and basic junk. I couldn't resist making a purchase of two attractive martini glasses, medium in size with cobalt blue stems, always a reminder of this delightful town.

THE GRAND CANYON

It was our last night staying at The Railway resort in Williams. Having swum in the pool for a couple of hours it was time for everyone to have an early night. Tomorrow we were off to The Grand Canyon. There was much anticipation, there was talk of who would be the first to spot a coyote or a chipmunk. There was even talk of a helicopter ride. The boys were not at all tired, which is par for the course when parents yearn for an early night. It was Josh who requested a story and Jake agreed, suggesting that the subject should be the Grand Canyon. Josh was fine with this as long as it didn't involve a helicopter ride. They also insisted that the story should feature the two recurring characters Jake and Josh.

With the boys tucked up in their bunks and Mum cross-legged on the floor, the story began.

A Once Upon a Time Story, The Grand Canyon

The Children, Jake and Josh, went to bed early that evening but were so excited about their forthcoming trip to the Grand Canyon that they struggled to fall asleep. This was for different reasons. Jake was thrilled about the possibility of a helicopter ride and the very thought of being in the sky hovering over not just any canyon but the Grand one at that, kept his thoughts racing. Josh, however, was looking forward to being the first one to spot a coyote, he did so hope it would be him, after all Mum and Dad had promised $5 to the first person who spotted one and he could do with the extra cash to buy another Star Wars model. He was, however, very anxious about the possibility of a forthcoming helicopter ride. He didn't want to go but didn't want to admit it and certainly didn't want his brother to find out he was anxious. Before too long both boys did eventually relax and become sleepy each with their individual thoughts... And dreams.

The boys found themselves being carried along by a soft warm breeze which was taking them over soft pine treetops and then across a huge orange and gold canyon which they guessed must be The Grand Canyon. They had never seen anything like it before, it was so very deep and wide. They awoke very relaxed and comfortable and were still in that twilight dreamy zone and were stretching awake when they discovered that they were rather high up a mountain sitting on and leaning against some very dusty rocks. This was puzzling – how on earth did they get up so high? Sensing they were not alone, they slowly turned and looked above them, realising they were being watched by what at first seemed to be a horned monster with staring eyes. They clung to each other, not daring to move. It was the horned creature that moved first, coming slowly and deliberately towards them, looking intently at each boy. As he got near to them, he nodded his head. Josh was less frightened now as he realised the monster had kind eyes and he immediately downgraded him from monster to creature status; after all, he had never heard of a monster that had such a caring face. Jake too was beginning to relax a little, his first thoughts of making a run for it gradually dissipating as he realised that he and his brother were not destined to become breakfast for a monster and his family. However, it was all such a puzzle. How did they come to be on the edge of the canyon and so high up? They needed some answers.

The creature stared at both boys. "I can help you with your puzzle," he said. "You see I needed you and you came here on the night breezes, although it was not quite as easy as that as I had to get the permission and agreement of the forest committee which is overseen by the Douglas Fir trees who, incidentally, having agreed, helped make it happen."

The brothers turned to each other and stepped away,

making sure they were out of earshot. Something was happening here that was unlike anything they had ever known – forget about forest committees, and Douglas firs, the mystery was that they were somehow communicating with a creature that wasn't actually speaking, and yet they knew its exact meaning. Dr Doolittle this wasn't.

They agreed they needed to know so much more, like who and what he was, a name at least, and why were they needed. Josh also wanted to know more about the canyon itself and how it got there – did someone or something, maybe dinosaurs, dig a big hole? They had a feeling this was one of those times they needed to be patient, which wasn't their thing at all, but hopefully the creature would reveal all.

The creature nodded his head as though he understood all their thoughts. "OK, I will answer all your questions in time," he communicated, "but first, let me introduce myself. I was given the name Kamali, there is nothing very special about me. My name means Spirit Guide and humans call us Big Horned Sheep. We have inhabited this Canyon for many years, but our numbers are slowly declining, and each year there are fewer and fewer of us. We love living here in this desert climate and if you look at our feet you will agree they are small and nimble, great for steep and rocky terrain." Picking up on a thought from Josh he went on, "We eat lots of plants and shrubs and need little water."

Josh wondered if they all look like him with his curly

horns, and Kamali explained. "I am a Ram and all Rams have curly horns, the females or Ewes have short horns which are less curved. I am the dominant one of my herd of ten."

Jake asked what that meant exactly.

"Well, it is the custom of the Rams to fight each other, we charge at one another with our horns and the loser is the one that retreats first. We do this prior to the mating season which gives us an authority over the Ewes."

Jake was curious to know who their predators are.

Kamali said, "Our lambs need protection when they are born from most animals and large birds in the forest, including coyotes, bobcats and even golden eagles. We watch out for bears, wolves and cougars. We have to be careful of the many snakes in the Canyon, and of course humans are the most dangerous of all. The worst humans leave many plastic packages lying around which we can eat by mistake, many of our sheep have suffocated because plastic gets stuck in the throat and they cannot get rid of it; it is a most horrible death."

Both boys shuddered to think what damage can be done by human thoughtlessness and became deep in thought.

It was Josh who broke the silence and came straight to the point, wanting to know why two boys were needed – after all what could they possibly be able to do – and he was also intrigued to know how Kamali was commutating with them.

"Communication between us all in the Canyon and forest is easy," said Kamali. "We receive from each other thoughts and feelings and this is our way of talking, just like we have been doing together."

'Wow,' Josh wondered, 'why can't humans talk together in that way, there would be a lot less noise.'

Kamali thought that they could but they probably don't trust their own ability to do so therefore they have taught themselves another system using sounds.

"As for needing the two of you, I really do. My herd live just one mile away high on the hill over where you can see that rocky mass. Yesterday, while I was away there was a loud rumble and I returned to find there had been a landslide, trapping my herd in between the rocks. The Ewes are all due to give birth within a few days and if they cannot be rescued the lambs will be born and will not survive."

Jake just sighed and wondered how on earth he and his brother could possibly help. They needed to get to the site fast. Kamali suggested that the boys should ride on his back. Josh being the smallest climbed on first and grabbed Kamali's horns, Jake followed and held onto Josh for the bumpy ride ahead. When they arrived, they could see the herd clinging to the rocks. The boys looked at each other, shaking their heads, they could see the only way out for the herd was to climb over those rocks, yet that was impossible because the loose rocks would only collapse again the moment any weight was put on them. Josh suggested the rocks would be made safe by cementing in the gaps, but realised it would be impossible to get cement to the rocks in time. With the same thought Jake wondered if the gaps could be secured using foliage. Kamali was listening with interest to this idea, because if somehow they could make a secure wall, the herd could climb to safety albeit with a bit of help. The three of them were so lost in their thoughts they didn't see the snake slithering up beside them but a second later all three heard it. A most peculiar sound as though it was rattling along the path. It was a very scary sound, which seemed to be coming from its tail. Jake shouted to Josh and Kamali to look out, and suggested they very slowly move away with no sudden movements. The snake rose up, rearing his rather thick, broad diamond shaped head and stared at the two boys. 'Ah humans,' it thought, 'and young ones at that, I've no intention of wasting my precious venom on those two, besides it's winter.'

The boy's minds went blank but Kamali explained that during the winter months snakes become slow and less active. Kamali was curious to learn what had brought the snake to this place at this time of year. The snake quickly explained that he and his friends were sheltering and resting in the rocks and crevices when they heard a huge rumble and they all tumbled to the bottom of the canyon. It wasn't very pleasant at all, but he was now looking for a new resting place for everyone to enjoy the relaxing winter months. Kamali said he understood and told his own story of his herd, which was stuck behind all the loose rocks, and his fears of losing his lambs. The snake started making rattling sounds again and suggested that although he could sympathise it was not his problem. This couldn't care less attitude infuriated the boys, Josh in particular, and he certainly made his feelings clear to the snake. He was no longer frightened of a rude snake who insisted on making an awful noise just to intimidate others, and who shares this beautiful canyon which is his home, with other creatures he has relied on in the past, sometimes for company, sometimes for food. What gives him the right to just walk away without even trying to help? The snake's head seemed to shrink back slightly making him look a little guilty.

"Oh all right," he said, "no need to go on so, but I don't know what I could possibly do that will help, but let's get one thing straight, I am not rude."

Jake thought that was a matter of opinion and was rather proud of his brother for standing up to the snake. He immediately suggested that the snake stop making that dreadful rattling noise.

The snake patiently explained that as a rattle snake, the noise comes from his tail. "I have highly modified scales," he said, "which I am very proud of. I can't help making a noise – after all, that is how I protect myself from predators. I just rattle along, that's what I do."

It was now the turn of the boys to feel a little guilty.

Kamali was quietly amused with the banter but suggested they all try hard to think of a solution to the problem as time was running out. They thought, and they thought and thought again.

It was Jake who had an idea and he turned to address the snake but realised he didn't know its name, so he asked. The snake was embarrassed as he didn't want to reveal his personal name.

"Oh, come on," the boys said; they were now very eager to know. "You know all our names and we promise not to laugh."

But they did laugh!

His name was Ratty. Jake quickly smothered his laugh and moved on, asking questions about Ratty's flexibility and strength. Surprised, Ratty demonstrated his flexibility by winding himself around a few dead tree branches and went on to climb a rock. "As for strength, what had you in mind?" Jake explained that it's an idea that Josh had about cementing the rocks together "and I was wondering if you and maybe some of your friends could be the cement. You would have to weave your way through the loose rocks horizontally thus holding them in place and others could weave their way vertically which would secure a wall. The ewes could then climb their way back to safety."

Kamili looked towards the Douglas firs, closed his eyes and gently nodded. "I think it's an ingenious idea." He turned to Ratty. "How many of your friends can you find?"

He shrugged and said, "Hundreds if you want."

So a plan was determined at last and Kamali dared to think

about the birth of his lambs.

He looked on as the boys with Ratty and his friends got to work. The two children were giving orders and direction whilst the snakes were weaving through rocks, rubble and the odd dead tree branch to produce a wall good enough for the herd to climb back to safety. It took time, a whole day in fact, and when nightfall came there was nothing to do but wait for first light, the snakes seemingly comfortable in their rocks and crevices whilst Kamali and the children huddled together for warmth under a rock face. As soon as the sun rose, Kamali was up and slowly and surely made his way down the wall towards his herd. He found the Ewes frightened but so happy to see him and he called to the boys to get ready. It was their job to guide the Ewes to the top and into a safe cave they had found, where they could happily give birth. The climb took time, but the ascent was accomplished around midday. No sooner had the Ewes arrived when the birthing started, and what a sight to see. The lambs were the cutest. The boys nearly forgot about Ratty and his friends, but later learned that they had decided to stay in the rocks and crevice wall for a while longer.

Word soon got around the herd of how the boys with their ingenious ideas saved the lives of them all, with of course the help of Ratty and his friends. Kamali then remembered how Josh really wanted to know all about the canyon. So rather that make their way home, they decided to stay one more night with Kamali, his herd and the lambs.

They gathered that evening in the cave with the Ewes and their lambs and there was much discussion over what to name each lamb. The first born if it was a boy was always called Sakima, meaning chief. The name Bly, meaning tall, was a favourite of one of the Ewes as her lamb stood taller than the rest, Miakoda for a little girl was a popular name as was Lonan meaning cloud and Lenmana meaning flute girl. Final decisions would be made later and when Kamali walked in the den, a silence fell over all the Ewes, and the lambs snuggled up to their mothers.

Kamali chose Una, his favourite of the Ewes, to join him at the front of the herd while he gave thanks to the forest for the help and guidance he had received and he thanked in particular the Douglas Firs for bringing Jake and Josh safely to him. He also thanked the rattle snake community for making the rescue at all possible.

Kamali explained to the herd that Josh wanted to know more about the Grand Canyon as he had wondered if someone years ago had dug a huge hole deep into the ground to create the canyon. The Ewes smiled and twittered fondly amongst themselves, envying the simplicity of youth, and it was Una who began to explain the wonders of the Grand Canyon. She fully understood why Josh should think such a thing as the canyon was over one mile deep and is a very special place. It stretches as far as the eye can see, hundreds of miles in fact, and in places is ten miles wide. It is extremely old, but not nearly as old as the wind. Josh was unsure how old the wind was but didn't like to say. Una went on to explain that a long time ago the Colorado river carved out the Grand Canyon, and each time it rains, water runs down the canyon walls and washes tiny pieces of rock and sand with it. That's called erosion. Erosion also happens when the river at the bottom rushes between the canyon walls and washes sand and rock into the river. The Grand Canyon is getting wider and deeper all the time. Kamali joined in and explained that the Colorado river had started making the Canyon about 17 million years ago. Wow, thought Josh, that makes the wind very old indeed. Jake wanted to know if anyone had ever lived in the Canyon and was surprised to learn that about 3,000 years ago it was inhabited by Peublo Indians who used caves as shelter and carved out rooms which were used for storing grain. The boys didn't think they could possibly live in caves so far away from everything they knew, but they also thought what a different life it could be living with all these wonderful animals.

By now Kamali, the herd, the lambs, and the boys were all very sleepy and curled up together for warmth for the night ahead. Kamali closed his eyes and connected with the forest and the firs, and quietly whispered a big thank you and sadly, quietly said goodbye to the boys...

The next morning

The next morning after breakfast we set off on one of our shortest journeys, only 51 miles to the South Rim of the Grand Canyon. It took us about an hour via the Historic Route 66. Our campsite was called the Grand Canyon Camper Village and it was the most basic of sites so far, but workable. However, we didn't take favourably to the facilities and decided to use our own bathroom which was more than adequate. The weather didn't help as we noticed the temperature had dropped from around 70 F to 46 F at this higher altitude. Having hooked up and connected the propane for the central heating, we then prepared for cold weather bringing out the cosy anoraks, hats, gloves, and scarves. After this we found we still had a good half day in front of us to go and explore. We unhooked Tobie and drove to the South Rim carpark of the visitor's centre, always a good place to start in the National Parks. We made our plan for the afternoon and drove east to the Desert view trail which, as the name suggests, has several viewing spots.

We started at the Grand Viewpoint, which was spectacular, then on to Moran Point and finally Navajo Point. Here you feel you are on the rim of the world with views over the Canyon of more than 7,000 feet, and rock colours of golds and crimsons setting off the cool blues of the Colorado river. We walked all around and headed for the amazing Watchtower built in the 1930s using Hopi Indian tribe labour. Inside there were many paintings and objects depicting Hopi legends. Interestingly, the Watchtower was designed by one of the first female architects in the United States, Mary Jane Colter. It was crafted to represent the history of the area, built with native stone and was modelled after the ancient Hopi village of Oraibi. When finished it became living quarters for the Hopi craftsmen and it was where they sold, and to this day sell, the Indian made arts and crafts and other types of souvenirs. We enjoyed looking through all these handcrafted items, particularly the handmade rugs, pottery, jewellery, paintings, which included sand paintings, kachina dolls, and so much more.

We particularly loved the sand paintings and learning about the history. Unfortunately, the original sand paintings do not exist, as they were never made as art forms. Instead they were part of a healing process created by the medicine men of the tribe by pouring natural coloured sands to create pictures. The sand painting may contain an image of the holy people called the yeibicheli and often the medicine man would ask the yeibicheli for help, ensuring the accuracy of the painting. During a ceremony the patient would sit on the painting. The sand painting serves as a portal for the healing spirits and through this painting the patient absorbs healing energy. After the successful removal of the illness, the painting is destroyed as it is believed to now contain the illness and is toxic. Once destroyed, the illness is demolished.

This entire ceremony was usually completed within twelve hours. Nothing was ever written down and all this medical knowledge was handed down by mouth from generation to generation. The art form today is relatively new. The artist first must learn how to adhere sand to canvas. Of course, the sand used today is mainly bought over the counter and applied by tube.

Catching our eye were the Kachina dolls, which were originally carved from cottonwood root by the Hopi people and were a type of Spirit being. The boys were fascinated by a beautiful display of Dream Catchers, which fired their imagination. Jake told us the story of the Spider Women whose Indian name was Asikikaashi, who was from the Ojibwe tribe and it was her job to take care of the people and in particular the children. But as this tribe expanded and moved further away it was believed the spider women could not take care of all the children. It was the mothers and grandmothers who had the idea of hanging webs which were made of netting, around the cradles and beds of all their young offspring. It was believed that the webs caught any harm that might be in the air just as spiders' webs catch and hold everything that comes in contact with them. Traditionally made from a willow hoop onto which is woven a web, beads, charms and feathers are then sewn on. Today people still buy these for their children and grandchildren in the hope of catching all the bad dreams and letting the good dreams pass through.

We were hoping that it would work for Josh, who sometimes awoke with nightmares. The boys chose one each and hung them on their bunks. Even today Dream Catchers are never far from their beds.

The next day we made our way back to the visitors' centre to make plans for the day. We decided to look around the Grand Canyon Village before making our way along the West Rim Drive to Hermits Rest, a seven-mile walk or drive. The road is closed to all private vehicles most of the year, but a shuttle bus runs frequently.

The Village is the obvious hub of the Canyon, offering board and lodging from the most basic of lodges to more elegant hotels. There is also a more basic campground further away in the pine forest. The village also offers many restaurants, again from basic inexpensive cafes to the more fine dining establishments where no shorts or jeans are allowed. A general store carries groceries and camping equipment. As we made our way to the bus stop, we were surprised and uneasy as most parents would be when we realised the fencing around the edge of the canyon trails was either inadequate or non-existent. Not safe for adults never mind active children. There are many deaths per year with people falling over the edge and a mile down to the bottom of the canyon. Keith took charge of Josh and I took Jake's hand as we walked to catch the bus along Hermit Rd. Our first stop was Hopi Point, where we gazed at canyon views taking in the

Colorado river to the west. We walked on the trail to Mohave Point, which was nearly a mile, again with spectacular views. We then walked another mile or so onto The Abyss. It was on this trail walk that Jake took me to one side and to my surprise complained that I was spoiling the adventure for him. I looked at him in total astonishment. He explained that he was nearly choking because I not only had grip of his hand but also his collar. He assured me he wasn't intending to go near the edge. I realised he was right, but the thought of those sheer drops terrified me. Keith and I made a quick decision and swapped boys. I was far more comfortable with Josh who was walking as far away from the edge as possible. Poor Jake.

The view from The Abyss point was impressive as it provided almost vertical views down to the canyon, looking down into Monument Creek. We saw a few backpackers on their way down to what is a popular spot for camping. We suspected they would be hiking for most of the day so that they could reach the much warmer temperatures down at the bottom of the canyon. It was here that Josh spotted the first Coyote, light brown in colour with a narrow nose, pointed ears and a black tip on his tail which was held down. He was over the moon and not long after that he spotted a squirrel and Jake spotted a large lizard, which we thought might be the collared lizard.

We decided to take the bus to the next Point which was Prima Point. We were told this was the best place on the Rim to see and hear the river. Sometimes you can hear the splash and grind of granite rapids below echoing up the canyon walls. Alas we didn't hear them this day. We walked to the next trail, Hermits Rest, which was a paved trail, easier on the mind as well as the legs, as the other trails were on rough terrain. This was about a mile from Prima point. Mary Colter, the American architect, built Hermits Rest in 1914 to look like an old miner's cabin complete with a giant fireplace and front porch. Today it has a gift shop and small café, and it was here we rested and enjoyed a hot drink and some food, also spotting more wildlife – this time, rock squirrels. We set off, having decided to walk all the way back, but after about a mile with little warning we found ourselves in the middle of a rainstorm. The decision to take the bus back to the village was made for us. We were very thankful to arrive back at Tobie and to drive back to the warmth of our coach.

The next day we leisurely made our way through the forest to the Helicopter pads ready for the trip around the canyon. Josh was putting on a brave face but clearly was uneasy about a helicopter flight. We gave him the option of staying on the ground with one of us, but he decided to come. Maverick Tours had insisted we arrive one hour before take-off as we all had to be carefully weighed. We were given lockers for bags etc and by the time we had coffee and sorted ourselves out we were ready to go. Jake was sitting at the front next to a rather large lady who was from Scotland. I was next to her with a Norwegian gentleman to my other side. Behind was Keith next to the window with Josh next to him and a couple from Arkansas. The pilot introduced himself and gave us an idea of what to expect when in the air, and explained a few safety features including the headphones we each had to wear. He gave us the route and assured us the weather was perfect for the canyon ride. We were ready for take-off. It was extremely noisy. Up we went over the Kaibab National Forest where we spotted a herd of deer. Seeing the area from such a height put the huge forest into perspective, it seemed to go on for ever, then, without warning, the huge forest came to an abrupt end and we found ourselves over the deep canyon. It was like being at the top of a large Ferris Wheel without any support. All our stomachs were in turmoil. Josh, next to Dad, had his eyes shut and to be honest at this point my conscience was niggling – should children be put into this dangerous situation? However, it was Jake's gasp of WOW and his obvious delight that bought me back to the realisation of what a privilege this was. We could see a mile down the deep sided canyon where the Colorado river had slowly carved its way through. The colours changed with the light but on that day the top was a crimson red, the middle a mustard yellow and the bottom looked very dark. The pilot pointed out some hikers making their way downwards and I'm not sure that I wouldn't have changed places with one of them given the opportunity, but as we flew around the canyon I relaxed and started enjoying the ride. Glancing behind me I saw Keith was holding Josh's hand, but I couldn't see his face and I dared to hope he was enjoying it. There were a few cotton clouds above us that you felt you could touch. We flew down into the canyon for a while and then back up and around. You could clearly see the ten miles width and the two hundred and seventy seven miles length of the canyon; it seemed to never end. I was getting really comfortable when the pilot announced we were returning across the pine forest and this was when Josh asked his dad if now would be a good time to open his eyes. Back on the ground, we all realised what an experience it really was – Josh, smiling, agreed.

Boys at the edge of the canyon

Joshies Grand Canyon spottings

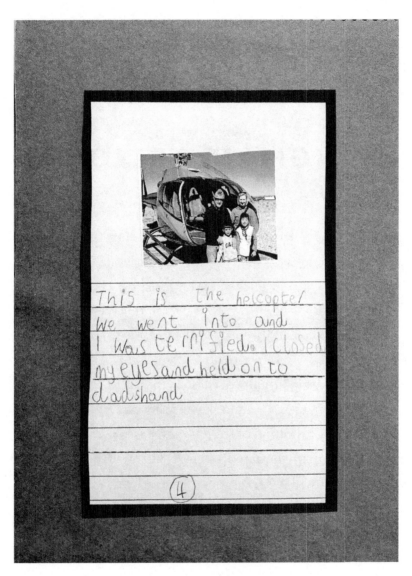

Joshies scary helicopter trip

KINGMAN ARIZONA

We have often heard the expression 'it's a gender issue' – well, here in Kingman Arizona I can offer an excellent example of such. This location was chosen because of accessibility to the town of Oatman, the West Rim of the Grand Canyon, and the heart of the historic Route 66. Keith's enthusiasm, however, throughout our three night stay at Kingman was not for any of these great places but for a truck stop. To be honest I would have (deliberately) forgotten all about it had it not have been for the passionate reminder I received from my husband when discussing Kingman, so for this reason I will try and execute as much fervour in writing about the 'Truck Stop' as possible.

Nowadays the word Truck Stop often conjures up images of rednecks, roughs, and those who favour hardwear worn about their person, but this has been replaced with Travel Plazas and Shopping Centres which attract not only the professional drivers but also everyday motorists. For the professional drivers they are used mainly for overnight stops; motorists use them for the usual fuel stops, bits of shopping and food. For the overnighters these stops offer every convenience possible which are often free when purchasing a certain amount of fuel. The facilities include a TV lounge and games room, showers, self-service laundry, truck waste, business services, Wi-Fi in restaurants, ATM, postal services, movie rentals, small grocery stores, wide selection of truck and trailer maintenance products, service centre which performs routine maintenance and repairs, tyre sales, puncture repairs, well-lit 24 hours security plus CCTV and truck and R V washes. Not sure all the above impressed Keith as much as the RV wash. Baystar, at this time, was filthy and in need of a clean. The vehicle washing machines were huge, but the impressive part came from the work of six men, who remarkably climbed up the sides of the coach with cloths, brushes and hoses. The whole escapade took around fifteen minutes, and Baystar at the end shone. Keith seemed fascinated with the overnight facilities offered to the commercial drivers and had a good look around, as well as a good look at some of these huge 65 foot long beasts which can weigh 75,000 pounds when loaded and can average over 10,000 miles per month. At night they plug a large AC into the cab; each cab is very compact with a sleeping section, a good size bed, with cupboards and hanging space, a fold down table often with chairs, a pantry mini fridge, microwave and many enjoy TV, DVD etc. Combine their facilities with the ones on offer at the stops, these truck drivers are looked after well and it is not such a bad living.

This truck stop was opposite our campsite, Blake Ranch. We too had good amenities with private bathrooms, which were spotless, plus places for the boys to run around so we had no complaints, but unfortunately the proprietors did and they were about our boys. The grievance was delivered by a member of staff knocking on our door complaining that Jake and Josh were playing in the dirt by some trees; we of course apologised and advised the boys to play elsewhere, but never did understand exactly what they had done that was so wrong.

The day we had put aside for our visit to Oatman was the only day of our American trip when I happened to be unwell, so the three boys ventured forth without me.

Oatman is now a ghost town and very popular with tourists. It was originally an old mining town that became a flourishing mining centre when in 1915 two miners struck a ten-million-dollar gold find and within a year the population grew to over three thousand five hundred. It was named after Olive Oatman, kidnapped as a young girl by an Apache tribe, sold to the Mojave Indians and eventually rescued in 1857.Unfortunately, the population and mining boom was short-lived when in 1920 a fire spread throughout the town, burning down many of the shacks. About three years later the main mining company, United Eastern Lines, shut down operations for good. Oatman survived by catering to travellers on the old US Route 66. This changed again in the 1960s when the new interstate 40 became the main route. This was when Oatman finally nearly died.

However, it is now an authentic old Western Cowboy Town catering to tourists. It is full of wild Burrows which are descendants of the old gold mine mules, they kick and they bite and some at night go back to the hills to sleep. The boys witnessed a staged cowboy gunfight which they loved as they felt quite part of the scene and took as many photos as possible. The Oatman hotel has celebrity status – built in 1902, it is one of the oldest adobe structures in the Mojave County, and it not only housed many of the miners, many scoundrels but also film stars and politicians. The backdrop of the town has been used in movies such as Foxfire and Edge of Eternity. In 1939 Clark Gable and Carol Lombard spent their honeymoon at the hotel, Gable returning often, it is said, to play poker with the locals, enjoying the solitude of the desert. The honeymoon suite is still an attraction to visitors.

Our next excursion was to the West Rim of the Grand Canyon, better known as the Glass Sky Walk. A very enjoyable ride until we hit the famous Dolan Springs Diamond Bar Rd, a 20-mile drive but the last 9 miles was tricky. An unpaved loose stone and dirt rutted road. Tobie was a truly off-road jeep but even so she was truly struggling; it wasn't just the fact that every bone in our bodies was shaking but every nut and bolt and body part of Tobie was rattling. We kept stopping and checking that nothing had fallen off, Keith showed tremendous patience and skill as he slowly drove the jeep, but it seemed we were sitting on top of a pneumatic drill. We made it, but where were we?

The Skywalk is not located at the Grand Canyon proper but at Grand Canyon West on the Hualapai Indian Reservation, approximately halfway between Las Vegas and the Grand Canyon south rim, or a three-hour drive from Las Vegas via the Hoover Dam. The Hualapai (pronounced wall-uh-pie) people, or the people of tall pines, have lived in the south west for untold generations; the reservation of 1,000,000 acres was established in 1883.The Skywalk, commissioned and owned by the Hualapai tribe was opened and unveiled in March 2007 by astronauts Buzz Aldrin and John Herrington who was the first enrolled member of a Native American tribe to fly in space. The Skywalk is basically a platform over the edge of the Canyon, the deck being made of 4 layers of low iron glass. It is a Cantilever shaped glass walkway suspended 4,000 feet above the canyon floor and it extends 70 feet from the canyon's rim. It was the idea of Las Vegas businessman David Jin, who was encouraged by a Vegas design company. What is a cantilever bridge? Simply, it is a long bar that is fixed at only one end to a vertical support and is used to hold a structure such as an arch, bridge or shelf in position. The Skywalk is said to be able to hold the weight of a dozen fully loaded 747s and sturdy enough to withstand winds up to 100 miles per hour, although no more than 120 people are allowed on the structure at any one time.

We eventually arrived at the entrance, well shaken and well stirred, but ready for some excitement. After paying our entrance fee, having placed our belongings in lockers, we were each given foot coverings designed to protect the glass floor. These shoes reminded us all of the surgical footwear worn by surgeons during operations, not a pretty picture, but cameras were banned which was a small consolation. We were all terrified as we ventured forth on the glass flooring, holding hands but marvelling at the views all around and bravely looking down, feeling suspended in time as well as space. Alas it was over too quickly, and after we had all recovered the boys went to investigate the Indian tepees.

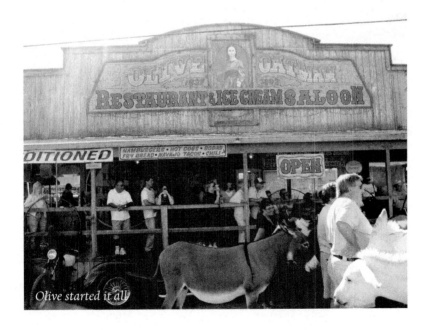

Olive started it all

Skywalk

We didnt get to meet her

The Hualapai tribe

UTAH

I think this maybe a goodtime to mention Tobie. Both Keith and I were quite concerned. We knew that something was wrong mainly because of the awful sound that came from the engine when first engaged. I can only compare this horror of a noise to fingernails scraping on an old-fashioned blackboard. We were not sure what the problem was, but knew that Tobie needed to be checked over sometime soon. Until then, however, she was perfectly safe being towed behind the coach.

The drive to Utah ranks high on our Best Journey list, taking us from Kingman, Arizona to St George, Utah. We were aiming towards the US-93 entering Nevada close to Las Vegas, then heading for I-15 towards Salt Lake City and then passing back through Arizona before entering Utah. The high ranking of this drive, apart from the scenery changes, was mainly because of the crossing over the famous Hoover Dam. We had a journey ahead of us of approx. three to four hours which didn't include stops, therefore some background knowledge about this well-known Dam seemed to be the order of the day, and the boys were eagerly awaiting hearing about it and seeing it.

It is a concrete arch-gravity dam located in the Black Canyon of the Colorado River on the border between Arizona and Nevada. It is an ingenious design. It works by one side, i.e. Lake Mead, pushing against the dam, creating compressive forces that travel along the great curved wall. The canyon walls push back on the other side, counteracting these forces. This action squeezes the concrete in the arch together, making the Dam very rigid and it cannot be pushed over. It was constructed during the time of the Great Depression resulting in a massive effort involving over five thousand workers. Unfortunately, over one hundred men lost their lives during the construction.

Since 1935 the Hoover Dam and Lake Mead have provided flood control, irrigation, drinking water and power to communities in the Desert, transforming the Southwest into production farmland and thriving communities. It was also originally built to protect farmland in Southern California from flooding from the Colorado River.

The Hoover Dam has long been recognised nationally and internationally as one of the world's greatest engineering and construction achievements.

We were just finishing off our lesson as we approached this famous dam. The boys enjoyed facts such as that it was built with 4.5 million cubic yards of concrete, enough to build a two-lane highway from Seattle to Miami. It also used 88 million pounds of plate steel. It is over 726 feet high, the base is 660 feet thick and it is 1244 feet long at the crest.

As Baystar slowed down at the top of the road leading down to the dam proper, Keith was asked by some very official looking armed men, to manoeuvre into a lay bay at the side of a checkpoint. These men demanded to enter and search our coach and ordered us to present our passports. Being a Brit I don't think I will ever get used to people carrying guns and I was most uncomfortable that arms were being brought into our home. The men then checked all the outside bays and lockers including the propane tank and generator lockers, presumably looking for explosive devices. When they confirmed us as a harmless family of Brits, we were rewarded with a smile and nod as they left the coach, which was a great relief especially as I fall into the category of those very ridiculous individuals who always feel guilty in the presence of Police or Customs officers.

The journey from then on to our destination, which was St George in Washington County, Utah, was quite spectacular as we watched the backdrop colours change from grey browns to reds. We checked into our new campsite, Mc Arthurs Temple View, and noticed signs welcoming back 'Snow Birds'. We learned for the first time that "Snow Birds" refer to the Canadian RV-ers who wish to escape the harsh Canadian winter weather in exchange for the warmer climes of the Utah winter. We drove into our pull through site which had a patio with table and chairs. As soon as the slides were out and all facilities engaged, we went to "case the joint" as the boys loved to say. The site catered for tourists like ourselves and also permanent residents who lived in their mobile home houses. These houses can be very luxurious and are not to be compared to caravans. They are referred to as mobile simply because they can be moved if required. We found the swimming pool and Jacuzzi, which were both heated, a good games room with billiards, a children's games room, a horseshoe pit and shuffle board courts, exercise room, lounge and a large laundry. The shower facilities were also nearby. We had found another very good site. The views from our parking spot were truly magnificent, showing the red of the mountains with white snow caps in the far distance, whilst on the other side a large D could be seen denoting Dixie land. A Mormon Temple sat prominently in the backdrop. The area which is fondly known as Utah's Dixie came about because the early Mormon settlers tried to grow cotton in this area, alas unsuccessfully, but the name Dixie has remained.

We crossed the road and found a shopping area. Needing a few provisions, we commenced the food shopping. Keith decided to find a garage where we could get Tobie fixed. The supermarket itself was fairly large, although not up to the American large we had become used to, but certainly more than big enough for our requirements. As we were finding our bearings wandering from aisle to aisle we almost bumped into what we thought was a film set. A group of about fifteen women plus the same number of children all seemed to be wearing period costume. We also noticed three or four men hanging around the checkout area. I am not sure where my original thoughts came from – after all why would a film with a cast wearing period costumes be shooting in a modern supermarket? The penny dropped eventually: this group were Amish people, obviously doing the same as ourselves, food shopping. We tried hard not to stare but the boys were genuinely curious and it was a subject we would talk about later. I left the boys discreetly observing and went to look for wine and beer. I needed help to locate this and asked an assistant only to be told they didn't sell alcohol. When I asked the obvious next question, where can I go to purchase such items, the assistant seemed embarrassed as he looked in both directions before answering. In Utah no supermarkets are allowed to sell any form of alcohol; the State regulates its sale. All alcohol is sold in State Liquor stores, which are few and far between. The age for buying and consuming alcohol in this state is twenty one. Apparently this has been the law since 1935, not long after prohibition.

The main conversation over dinner that night was the Amish people and their traditions. I was surprised to learn that their history dates back to the 1600s in Switzerland and shares a Swiss-German ancestry with traditionalist Christian church fellowships starting as a reform group from the Mennonite movement. High in their values are rural life, manual labour and humility. It was an interesting discovery especially as our own Baystar coach interior was made by the Amish people, carpentry being one of their special skills. They migrated to the US as early as 1800, initially settling in Pennsylvania. They attempt to preserve the elements of the late seventeenth century European rural culture, trying hard to avoid most of the modern-day traits. This is achieved mainly by isolating themselves as much as possible from American culture. They have a set of unwritten behavioural rules which help them keep to the parameters of their faith. This is known as the Ordnung.

All Amish believe it is the will of God to have large families, which is the reason that the Amish are among the fastest growing populations in the world with an average of seven children per family. Their food is simple and as pure as possible, and they sell many of their foods in their own outlets; pies, pickles, bread mixes and desserts are always popular.

Many Amish children school in their own communities until they are about fourteen or fifteen, when they are deemed ready for work within their own environment. The schoolteachers are usually unmarried women from the local community. Both of our boys decided that the Amish life wasn't for them and they were not too impressed with the period clothing worn by the children.

Our next conversation that night was about Tobie. Keith had left the jeep in the capable hands of the garage manager who would take a day or two to locate the problem and advise. As we had no intention of going anywhere for the next few days it was not inconvenient at all, so we waited.

It always takes a few days to get comfortable in a new campsite, for example where to go for reception, remembering where the pool is located, where are laundry facilities, and of course getting used to the showers. We kept to our usual bathroom system with Mum accompanying Josh and Dad with Jake. On the way to the shower block on the first morning, Josh and I were almost open mouthed as we stared at the red mountain backdrop magnified by the morning light, a sight we were to enjoy every morning at St George. As we entered the ladies' shower block we found a group of old ladies in a state of undress, Josh smiled his famous smile of innocence and looked the other way. On hearing our English accents, the old ladies smiled at us and muttered between themselves as we selected our shower units which were side by side. I could hear words such as so cute, did you see those beautiful eyes, how polite. As every mum knows, these are the words we just love to hear said of our offspring, therefore my feathers were well and truly fluffed up as I stepped into the shower. Passing Josh a new bottle of shower gel under the cubicle, I began to enjoy a hot shower. Over the past few weeks I had got used to Josh singing in the shower. He had a lovely voice and so I wasn't really concentrating on what he was singing, I was more concerned about the amount of bubbles that seemed to be floating up into my cubicle from the direction of Josh's. Turning my shower off and wrapping up in my towel, I could hear voices saying 'did you hear that', 'really' and 'how old is that child?' I was beginning to feel uncomfortable with the tone of their voices when I heard Josh singing at the top of his voice "Gloria, Gloria, I wanna see more of ya" over and over again. As we left the shower block I remember smiling at the group of ladies who were sitting together sunning themselves outside, and suggesting to Josh that he cuts down on the American TV as the song came from the film Happy Feet.

Always lots to learn when we arrive at a new location and Utah was every bit as interesting as we thought it would be. The city of St George was chosen mainly because of its location. Snow Canyon, Bryce Canyon and Zion National Park were not too far away and all three were on our must-see list. It is situated in the south-western part of Utah close to the Arizona border, lying in the north-eastern most stretch of the Mojave Desert, one hundred and seventeen miles north east of Las Vegas, Nevada and about three hundred miles south-west of Salt lake City. The climate is described as sub-tropical Mediterranean desert, with long, hot, dry summers reaching over 100 degrees and an average low of 31 degrees in the winter. It claims typically 300 sunny days a year. The population of St George is around 75,000 and boasts the second fastest growing metropolitan area in the US.

Utah is nicknamed the Beehive State and joined the Statehood in 1896. The beehive does not refer to bees but is in honour of the Mormons, a religious group who were the state's first white settlers. The Mormons believe in working industriously and living together in close communities the same way bees do. It is said that on the very first day they arrived in 1847, they got straight to work ploughing and making ditches for water so they could farm Utah's dry land. The state capital is Salt Lake City and the lake itself is four times as salty as ocean water, making it almost impossible to sink in it. Utah itself is bordered by Colorado to the East, Wyoming to the Northeast, Idaho to the North, Arizona to the South and Nevada to the West. It also touches a corner of New Mexico in the Southeast. The Sego Lily is Utah's State flower and surprisingly the Seagull is the state bird. It is also home to the biggest dinosaur footprints in the world, made by a Hadrosaurid (duckbill) dinosaur. Enough for one day.

It was time to visit the garage and see if Tobie could be fixed. The garage manager was called as we approached, and we followed him into the workshop to hear the worst. He explained it was the fuel pump which needed replacing. Keith was surprised and explained that a new one had been fitted only a few months ago when we purchased the vehicle. The manager smiled and went to get the fuel pump taken from Tobie and showed it to us, suggesting that this was the original fuel pump which had never been replaced. He also suggested he would give us a written report that we could perhaps use to recover monies from the dishonest dealer who had lied about fitting a new pump. Not a word was uttered from my lips, but secretly I was quite pleased that my original instinct about the dirty fingernailed, false smiling dealer turned out to be correct. We collected Tobie two days later, all mended and back to normal.

A word about Laundry. American campsites make this easy and it can be quite a social event as I frequently experienced. It is easy because the washing machines and dryers are of a decent quality and they would certainly pass any fit for purpose test. The actual laundry rooms themselves are well designed with plenty of large machines and ample space for folding. This folding space is of the utmost importance since it is the folding of the articles from the dryer whilst warm that makes ironing redundant. Therefore, I became a great fan of American Laundries. Sunday mornings before the family arose seemed to be a good time as any to tackle the week's laundry. One particular Sunday morning, I encountered Jo who was an American who lived at the camp six months a year in one of the mobile homes. When Jo realised I was a Brit he couldn't wait to talk politics with me and asked me my opinion about the new Obama administration. Realising

Americans can be deeply passionate about politics, I carefully worded a reply about new directions and changes that could be good, but only time would tell. Jo nodded in agreement and then launched into a lengthy dialogue which comprised slave trading, Abe Lincoln, Martin Luther King, the civil rights movement, leading to Barack Obama. He tried extremely hard to convince me that he himself could not be blamed for the past and attempted to pursue the argument towards the African-American community and their responsibilities towards their own past. Being careful not to analyse Jo's thinking, I quickly moved the subject towards a more neutral topic – the weather – and left political debate behind. After all, it was a Sunday morning and I needed to concentrate on the folding process.

Time to go for a drive and test Tobie's new fuel pump. We found ourselves travelling north out of St George into the most amazing scenery we had ever seen. The desert colours of reds and pinks merged into creamy whites and it was a soft desert wilderness of ancient lava flows, deep canyons and sloping hills. There were adobe style houses and small communities dotted around. We found ourselves winding our way through this glorious backdrop and noticed Snow Canyon signs and were pleased to get our bearings. In fact, we were only nine miles out of St George. On entering the Canyon I realised I had left my handbag in the coach and Keith was without his wallet so the small entrance fee of six dollars would have been a problem if Josh hadn't picked up his pocket money on the "just in case" off chance of passing by a toy store, so without a doubt Josh saved the day for us all.

It seemed a great place for children to run and have adventures, and as soon as they saw the endless petrified sand dunes, they were off, and so were we, on an incredible walk.

Snow Canyon is a strange name to find in a dry hot desert, but in fact the name came from two prominent Utah leaders Lorenzo and Erastus Snow. The canyon itself has a long history of human use dating back as far as AD200 when Anasazi Indians inhabited the region, using it for hunting and gathering. Later, around AD1200, the canyon was used by the Paiute Indians. Much later, in 1850, it was rediscovered by Mormon pioneers whilst searching for lost cattle. It was originally named Dixie State Park, then renamed in honour of the Snows. The park itself is 7,400 acres of scenic desert tapestry, varying from red and white canyons carved from Navajo sandstone in the Red mountains, to volcanic cones, deep red sandstone cliffs, stunning twisted layers of rock and, of course, the petrified sand dunes.

How on earth did it come to be here and how long ago? Tiny grains of quartzite sand were transported by wind more than 183 million years ago and this covered most of what is Utah today. The sand lay in dunes up to 2,500 feet thick; these were eventually cemented into orange and white coloured stone. Over more time water carved its way deep into the sandstone, shaping the canyons. About one and a half million years ago and as recently as 27,000 years ago, some of the cinder cones erupted, causing lava to flow down into the canyons filling them with basalt and new canyons were eventually carved. We saw many desert plants including yucca, creosote bush, sage bush and many flowering and non-flowering cacti. Whilst we didn't see any wildlife apart from a few geckos, we learnt afterwards that this desert area is home to three endangered species: the Gila monster (lizard), the Peregrine falcon and the desert tortoise.

Our drive home took us in another direction. Whilst we didn't get lost, we found ourselves just outside the Biggest Loser Camp which did look pretty impressive, and was known to us because there was at the time much publicity about it and not all good. Anyhow we all decided Snow Canyon was someplace we would return to, which we did several times.

We were becoming part of the landscape, enjoying the warm late autumnal climate. The home schooling was continuing well, our location was comfortable, with all facilities nearby including a small old-fashioned cinema, which we used a few times. We were used to the boys grading the restaurants out of five with the average being 3.5, and we also got used to the compromise that comes with eating out in a family restaurant, that of whose favourite restaurant we would go to. Here in St George we found the ideal eating place to suit us all. Chuck-A-Rama. This restaurant was family orientated and served a buffet. Normally buffets are Keith's pet hate – he has always stated that the food on offer at buffets was invariably mediocre and stale and often pretentious. However, this restaurant was different, it was busy and efficient with friendly staff and good chefs, the food was replenished frequently therefore always fresh. Good food with a home cooked touch, it became a favourite of ours and frequented often.

By now we were quite used to seeing Amish people going about their usual daily routines and the boys no longer stared but smiled at the children who in return shyly returned their gestures. We also acknowledged the Mormon people visiting their churches, the men often dressed in white. I have to be honest, my knowledge of the Mormon religion was limited, therefore it was about time to lay to rest my ignorance of this religion and share it with all three males.

Often known as the American religion, it is relatively young and its ground roots are based on Christianity. It was started by Joseph Smith in 1820 in New York. He claimed to have seen visions from an angel and this angel led him to a buried book that was written on golden plates and these plates contained religious history of an ancient peoples. In 1830 Joseph Smith published what he said was a translation of the plates. Today this book is known as the Book of Mormon, named after Mormon the ancient prophet. Today the church is often referred to as The Church of Jesus Christ of Latter-day Saints and integrates well with American society. This was not always the case as in the early years a percentage of Mormons openly practised plural marriage, a religious form of polygamy and this was breaking State laws. Strongly believing in family and community, they devote much time and money to the church, developing many activities for all ages. They are all required to donate one tenth (tithe) of their income to the church. They totally shun alcohol, tobacco, tea and coffee and any addictive substance, and also shun addictive behaviour such as gambling. They practise a strict code of chastity. Their normal practices include studying the scriptures, fasting on a regular basis, attending Sunday worship, involving themselves in church programmes and activities on weekdays and where possible no work on Sundays. They believe strongly in standards such as personal honesty, integrity, law abiding, chastity outside opposite sex marriage, and fidelity within marriage. They promote a healthy lifestyle, their diet containing mostly natural foods and they eat meat moderately. The centre of the Mormon cultural influence is in Utah with about 30% of the world's population. There are around 5.5 million Mormons in the USA, the fourth largest religious group. The population around the world grew when missionaries were sent out after World War 2.

Our next trip was to investigate Zion National Park. We needed a break as home schooling over the past two weeks had been quite intense as we hit some of the more academic topics. This park was about an hour's drive and yet another spectacular one. The park is located close to the small town of Springdale, which boasts of being one of the twenty prettiest towns in the US with its five hundred and thirty inhabitants. Out of all the national parks visited, this was the most romantic, with a mixture of coniferous woodland, high cliffs, rivers and streams, coupled with the fragrances wafting from the Ponderosa Pines, Maple and Cottonwood trees and the sheer magnificence of the red high cliffs with water falling dramatically from them.

The boys soon got into the spirit of the park as we walked along one of the riverside trails, making their own boats out of floating pieces of bark, large leaves for the sails, and twigs tied together with rotting debris of stems and grasses. On the whole, these boats stood up well to the rapids with just a few occasions when repairs were necessary. This particular walking trail took us to the weeping rock, and it was a perfect day to walk the trail as it was comfortably warm. We found ourselves deep in the heart of Zion Canyon. The trail started at the Temple of Sinawava and we made our way through rough terrain at the side of the river, gradually climbing higher until we had a great view of the Virgin River and lush hanging gardens and trees. The Weeping Rock is an alcove cut by water into the cliff. Water seeps from the one hundred foot high cliff and falls like tears, forming a curtain across the front of the alcove. Delicate hanging gardens cling to the cliff face. Later we learnt that we had only explored a small fraction of the park as it is 229 square miles. Zion canyon itself is fifteen miles long and up to half a mile deep, with the Virgin River cutting through. Because of its four life zones, desert, riparian, woodland and coniferous, it is home to many plants, birds, mammals and reptiles. We had plans to return to this wondrous park, and so did the boys as they revealed they had secretly hidden their boats carefully in safe places to await their return.

It was obvious we were getting close to Halloween as the advertising, including TV commercials, and general hype was, for want of a better expression, in your face, extremely commercial, and very tacky, but an obvious and serious money-maker for retailers who were more than happy to give away cheap sweets to the children in the hope of enticing them into their stores. They wanted the parents to spend their hard earned cash on such nonsense as fake blood, rotten plastic teeth ready for penetrating the soft neck of a virgin, gaudy crosses, and fake garlic that looked and smelt like a rotten onion. It was not just the children's stores that were full of costumes, masks and candy, but when I saw frozen burgers and waffles in the shape of witches and pumpkins in the local supermarket it was quite a turn off. Also let's not forget the trendy upmarket group who couldn't get enough of the "eyeballs" which were fresh tiny scallops with fish eggs carefully placed on top and which wobbled under refrigeration. Something for everyone I suppose.

With all such going on it would be quite understandable for us to perhaps think that America owns copyright to this so-called pagan festival; however, there is nothing native American about Halloween. That can be claimed by the Celts who lived over 2,000 years ago. It was all to do with the Harvest Festival or Samhain Festival, a joyful festival which marked the death of the old year and the beginning of a new one, but, in the transition between years and for one night only, this was a night when the world of the dead crossed back into the living world to haunt and scare. So, just maybe, the American slant on Halloween is not so far from the truth.

So where did this leave us? Just the same as any American family, I guess, searching the stores with two enthusiastic boys trying to find the most ghoulish of masks and costumes, and boy did we find them. Josh's choice was an outfit that included a rubber grotesque mask that you wouldn't want to meet on a dark evening. Even worse was Jake's mask, which was more scientific. It came with a pump and this pump pumped blood over the face of the mask at any time he chose to use it, Disgusting was my verdict, but we had two very happy boys, well, three actually as Keith was getting into American Halloween the way the boys were doing it and I have to admit even I had a ludicrous mask.

In the evening the boys trick and treated in full costume around our home area and eventually ventured into the shopping mall where every shop was ready with their treats. I'm not sure where the tricking came into it, but Keith and I selected a café in the centre of all this activity and quietly enjoyed a cappuccino. We left a couple of hours later when the boys had had enough and were ready for a change, so we walked towards home. On the way we passed our local cinema which was showing Scrooge and we all decided this would make a perfect end to our American Halloween. The film and the day had been a great hit.

After Halloween we talked about Christmas, and cards, and we chose to make our own card this year with an obvious American theme; however, we needed to photograph the boys and opted to have this done professionally, and so we found a local photographer to do our boys justice. In the meantime we set about designing the card and waited for the photos to be developed.

Our final big adventure in this area would be Bryce Canyon and having chatted with a few locals we realised the temperature in the area of Bryce Canyon would be considerably lower, indeed a full twenty degrees lower and many of the campsites were now closed for the winter season. For this reason we decided to leave the coach in situ at St George and venture forth with Tobie, who was now running perfectly, and opted for the comfort of hotel life for a few nights. We chose Ruby's Inn both for location and charm as it was full of family history dating back to 1923 when Ruby's was first established. It was Reuben C Syrett who brought his family to the area, establishing a ranch close to where the hotel is today, and he became host to visitors to Bryce Canyon and set up a Tourists' Rest, later building a lodge. Today it is run by Reuben's grandchildren from his son Carl.

This was one canyon that everyone talked about favourably and with such enthusiasm we couldn't wait to find out more. Firstly, Bryce canyon is not a canyon simply because it was not formed in the usual way canyons are formed – that is, by the process of running water; it is formed by a freezing and thawing process. It is in fact the most spectacular collection of amphitheatres situated along the eastern side of the Paunsaugunt Plateau. Only being there or a photograph will really bring this magnificent beauty home in its full glory. Bryce Canyon National Park is small by National Park standards. It is said to have been inhabited around ten thousand years ago and some of the findings date back to the Basket maker Anasazi tribe. The first European American explorers visited as late as the late eighteenth and early nineteenth century. Mormon scouts visited the area in 1850 to assess its potential for agricultural development. It was The Church of Jesus Christ of Latter-day Saints who sent Scottish immigrant Ebenezer Bryce along with his wife Mary to settle in the area – it was thought that Ebenezer's carpentry skills would be useful. The family chose to live under the amphitheatre at Bryce Canyon and built themselves a wooden dwelling they called home. Bryce grazed his cattle in this area, building a road to the Plateau in order to retrieve firewood and timber. He also built a canal to irrigate his crops and water the animals. This area was to become known as Bryce's canyon by other settlers to the area.

Excitement was building up in us all as we headed onto the I-15 toward Bryce. The journey took around two and a half hours. As well as staring out at the scenery, which was beginning to take on the particular hues of Bryce, the boys were keeping busy in the back with a quiz on the safety of lightning in the canyon which was part of the Junior Ranger course for kids.

Ruby's Inn was everything we expected, a cosy ranchers Inn and more importantly warm as we were feeling the temperature change. We adjusted our clothing into more appropriate outer gear like anoraks and woolly hats and gloves. I even wore thick tights under my trousers, a first for a long time. So we ventured forth for our first glimpse of Bryce. I thought by now we were used to the typical colours of Utah, but the subtlety and depth and purity of colour that engulfed us at Bryce was unbelievable. Our view of Bryce Amphitheatre that lay before us was from Bryce Point; it was an ensemble of colour and perfectly sculptured shapes that only nature can achieve. We viewed this Amphitheatre from three other viewpoints, Sunset, Sunrise, and Inspiration Point. At the time we were all suffering from limited vocabulary and it was the first time that the word awesome was used in its correct context.

It was early evening when we returned to Ruby's and I remember luxuriating in a hot bath before dinner, and then later at the bar ordering a whisky. There is something comforting about a whisky on a cold evening; however, making the barman understand "without ice" wasn't so easy but on the third attempt having realised I was a peculiar Brit who preferred warm drinks he reluctantly removed the ice. The dinner that evening was a typical rancher's meal with the assortment of meats in particular steaks. It was not for the vegetarian, although vegetables were catered for in a small way. The boys, all three of them, tucked into steak options with sheer enjoyment and I did the same, but I have to say my enjoyment didn't just come from the food but from the sheer pleasure of not having to cook.

We were up early the next day, ready for the big adventure as we had decided we would walk down into the depths of the narrow canyons, agreeing between us to tackle the Navajo and Queens Garden trails. Jake, Keith and myself were well up for this, but we wondered about Josh who wasn't a natural walker; however, he eventually gave his consent – after all, he was only six and this trail was deemed moderately difficult and it was a round three and a half mile trip. So well done, Josh. We were well dressed for the occasion with hiking boots, layers for warmth, hat, gloves and scarves. We were ready.

Before we go any further it would be helpful to explain Hoodoos. Yesterday we were in awe of these magnificent, almost bizarre shapes which formed the Bryce Amphitheatre. These are in fact called Hoodoos, a trademark of the National Park. They are tall structures which form within sedimentary rock and protrude from the bottom of an arid drainage basin of Bad Lands. Hoodoos form over millions of years of erosion in areas where a thick layer of soft rock is covered by a thin layer of hard rock, helped by the continuous freezing and thawing conditions and wind. Hoodoos can be as small as five feet or as tall as one hundred and fifty feet. The Hoodoos at Bryce are found in the Park's horseshoe shaped Amphitheatres carved from the edge of the Paunsaugunt Plateau.

The obvious best way to see these Hoodoos was to hike down, hence the Navajo Loop and Queen Garden Trails. We started at what was named the Wall Street side, a narrow canyon with high walls, close to Sunset Point. The boys were in their element running ahead of us, heading down and down, hiding in all the nooks and crannies they could find. What we experienced was very different from the day before when we were looking down from the rim. Looking up you almost felt as though you were part of this amazing formation and at one with the landscape. Having caught up with the boys who were hiding in their lairs and who were on the lookout for foxes, bobcats, cougars, black bears, mountain lions and mule deer, we ventured through a narrow passage between towering rock arches which we learnt later were called Rock Fins, to find two hundred year Douglas Firs. I think these must be the most photographed trees in the world. The Native Americans found great uses for these trees. The bark was used for dye, pitch (resin) was used for sores, the boughs of the trees were used to make steam in the sweathouses, even the western pioneers found a use for the pine needles as they used them for a coffee substitute. Eventually, after finding and losing the boys a few times, we made our way into what is called the Queens Garden. We walked on to the other side and looked up at Queen Victoria's Hoodoo as she overlooked her garden fully in charge with all the majestic qualities you would expect. The boys played here until it was time to head on back –this time it was up and up, but we eventually made it without too much fuss from Josh who did extremely well.

We were fast coming to the end of our time in Utah. To be honest we agreed that we could spend at least another month here, but we learnt that the weather was turning colder in a few weeks and our plans were to spend Christmas in warmth. So just the boys' photos to collect before we moved on.

Boats sailing from the Virgin river to the gulf of Mexsico

Bryce Canyon 1

Hoover Dam

12th November

I had such an exciting day to day. First we drove to chilla rama (my favourite restrant). Then we went to The cinima and watched "A christmas carol". the story witten by Charles Dickens, is about an old man who was a Nasty and selfish man who was visited by three spirits that teach him the true meaning of the Holidays.

Jake's xmas carol diary

Ruby's inn Bryce Canyon

Zion National Park

ONCE APON A TIME...

When we arrived back at the coach the boys were still buzzing about Bryce Canyon and inevitably a Bryce Canyon story was requested. It had to include two boys called Jake and Josh who were on holiday. My stories were always spur of the moment, so I started the story and planned to continue it as we drove to our next stop, Lake Mohave. Here is that story.

The Pikhaupi Pikatoodoo

Once Upon A Time...there were two children, Jake who was nine years of age and Josh not too far behind at six years. It was summer time, the boys had just finished their last day of school and were so excited not just because there was no more school for a whole 8 weeks, but because the day after tomorrow they were flying long distance all the way to the United States of America to stay for a whole three weeks with their favourite Aunt Agatha and Uncle Brian. Oh boy were they excited. They loved their aunt and uncle and missed them so much when they moved to America. They didn't really understand why they had to move so far away but they did know it had something to do with Uncle Brian's job. You see, he is a Technician and America seemed to need an extra one. Anyway, they couldn't believe they were getting to stay with Aunt Agatha and Uncle Brian for a whole three weeks and without their mum and dad; wow, how great is that, and so grown up. Not that they didn't love their mum and dad, they really did, but at times they had funny ideas. For example, at meal times there was a rule which said they were not allowed to talk with their mouths full. OK, but Jake once forgot and Mum reminded him again. She said, "Jake, do not talk with your mouth full," so Jake stopped talking and thought for a second or two and very carefully took the food out of his mouth, holding it safely in his hands. He continued his conversation after which he returned the food to his mouth and finished eating. Mum and Dad just stared at him for some reason, open mouthed. Also, another silly rule, such a waste of time and energy, was, putting toys away every evening only to get them out again the next day. Sometimes Mum and Dad can be so embarrassing. Is it really necessary at school sports day to copy us kids in doing the obstacle race, for example? Didn't they realise the long tunnel tent was designed for kids' sizes not grownups? Most of the parents ended up wearing it. OH and boy do they panic, Jake and Josh remember the time when Josh played hide and seek without telling anyone, finding the perfect hiding place under the huge armchair in the lounge. He only went to sleep for a couple of hours and when he emerged refreshed and delighted with himself what did he find? Total panic, Mum had even called the security police – where on earth did they think he could possibly have got to?

Now they were pretty sure their aunt and uncle didn't have any such silly rules or ideas and they just couldn't wait to get there. With Mum's help they packed their suitcases, trying not to leave out anything important. They didn't know too much about America or where they were going except it is called Utah and Dad said Utah is in a bit of a state, or maybe it was Utah is a State; anyhow they were going to a place that was quite close to another place called Salt Lake City and this city had a huge lake with lots and lots of salt in it, which was great to swim in because the salt made you float but it's not good to drink. Jake had learnt all about that at school. They had seen lots of photographs of Utah and it looked very red and rocky which was great for climbing; also there is a canyon called Bryce Canyon. They knew this because of the photographs they had seen, and this canyon was very close to their aunt and uncle's house. In fact, their uncle told them on the phone that they call the canyon their back garden as it was so close. They just couldn't wait.

It was a long flight and the two boys never slept, not even for five minutes. Eventually the pilot announced that they had commenced their descent towards Cedar City Airport, which meant of course that they were soon to be landing. Their parents were fussing and making sure their seat belts were fastened and their bags were tidied up and put under their seats. It seemed to take forever, nevertheless they did eventually land and were soon together with their aunt and uncle. After many hugs and comments about how they had grown so much they said goodbye to their mum and dad who were flying off to somewhere else called Flooridoor, and after yet more hugs and promises to be good, the two boys were on their way with their aunt and uncle to their new home for three whole weeks in Utah.

They loved their aunt and uncle's house, which was full of nooks and crannies inside and on the outside; it was almost invisible as it seemed to disappear into the landscape. They loved their bedroom too as it was huge, plenty of room for two small boys and they had their own bathroom, but what they loved most about their room was that it had its own balcony overlooking Bryce Canyon. What a sight that was, the two boys had never seen such colourful and interesting rocks, some of them very conical looking, some of them had amazing twists and turns which led to pointed tops; they couldn't wait to play amongst them. Their aunt and uncle promised them that the next day when they were fresh and wide awake they would take them to visit Bryce Canyon.

The boys soon learnt that sometimes plans do not always happen as they are supposed to... It was during breakfast the following day that the plan began to fall apart. It started with loud banging on the door. Aunt Agatha opened the door to a rather fat young woman who was clearly distressed; in fact, she was screaming a bit. Jake who, being nine, knew all about these things, explained to his younger brother Josh that this rather fat lady was about to have a baby. Josh wasn't too bothered about this, but his brother seemed fascinated and volunteered to help. He found out that the lady concerned was a neighbour and she wasn't supposed to have her baby for another three weeks when her husband would be home, which meant it was down to Aunt Agatha to take charge. It was agreed that Uncle Brian would drive their car to the hospital and Aunt Agatha would help the neighbour in the back of the car. Incidentally, the name of the poor fat lady was Doris.

Uncle Brian told the two boys what was going to happen. They were to stay at the house and another neighbour would come and look after them until they got back from the hospital. They didn't think they would be more than a few hours or so, but the boys were to stay in the house and play. Under no circumstances were they allowed to leave the house. The neighbour's name was Dolores and she was to be totally in charge. Dolores arrived almost immediately and the children liked her instantly – they didn't know why, maybe it was her smile which seemed to stretch all over her face showing gleaming white teeth, or the way she just hugged them, one in each arm lifting them off the floor, or it could have been the enormous chocolate milkshake she made for them, so creamy with actual pieces of chocolate floating on top, it just couldn't get any better. Perhaps today was going to be OK after all. It was settled that the boys would play in their room while Dolores was busy around the house doing chores and such like to help Aunt Agatha.

They had lots of toys to play with and soon became engrossed with a huge box of Lego, creating their own shapes and characters. It was rather hot in their room which led Jake to draw the curtains back and open the door onto the balcony, which let in cool fresh air and a warm reddish light flooded the room. What lovely colours.

Josh noticed it first, although he was unsure what he was actually noticing, was it just the light that was making the rocks look as if they were moving? Jake couldn't see anything moving but did wonder if Josh had glimpsed the Mountain Lion they had heard so much about. They kept an eye out just in case, and suddenly they both saw something very alarming. The rocks started moving as if they were walking. They turned to stare at each other and then looked again. Oh my, the rocks were on the move. Yes, they were definitely on the move. What was going on? They didn't realise it at the time but what happened next, they would remember for the rest of their lives.

Some of the rocks had faces. Some of the rock formations seemed to be smiling at them. Some of these rocks were making sounds as if they were communicating with each other. The two boys just stood open mouthed, stunned. These majestic rocks, incredibly, moving before them with stately assertiveness was most humbling. Their colours with the midday sun shining upon them made them look as if they were carved out of pure gold. The boys just froze on the spot, waiting for more movement. They were not disappointed. The two further most rocks slowly turned towards them with expressions on their faces which reminded Jake of the Buddha in his kitchen at home, very wise and knowing. Just in front of them they noticed another rock moving and swaying slightly and before their eyes they watched as the base of the rock tugged and pulled away from the main rock with a loud crack, revealing a small individual pillar of rock with a sculptured face. This was not a rock anymore but clearly a creature, not human, nor animal, nor insect nor bird; nevertheless a creature with a kind face. The face was smiling at the two boys, and Josh noticed that the creature had two rather large front teeth giving it a very young look, which convinced him it must be a child like himself. They heard another crack as the base of the same rock pulled away again, and another slightly taller creature was revealed. This time the creature wasn't smiling but had a rather anxious look about it as it came hobbling over to the other one. The younger one was still smiling at the two boys as it pointed up at them and communicated something to its friend who nodded cautiously. Jake whispered to his brother that they should go and introduce themselves to make it clear that they were quite harmless and maybe they could make friends. Of course, if the boys wanted to make friends they couldn't keep calling them "it", they would have to start calling them "him" or find out if they had names. Josh was just about to mutter something about them not being allowed to go out when the older creature, if that's what he was, beckoned them down to meet them. Without any hesitation at all, Jake was over the balcony, running to meet them. Josh was close behind but was a bit concerned that they weren't supposed to leave the house and what would his aunt and uncle say? After all, they had promised.

When they met up, the boys stared at the creatures. They were surprised because they no longer seemed to be made of rock but instead they looked as if their whole bodies were made out of some sort of play dough. No one said a word for a while but just stared at each other. It was Josh who was the first to have the courage to speak and he politely introduced himself and his brother, explaining that they were on holiday and staying with their aunt and uncle. There was no answer and Jake wondered if the creatures spoke another language and asked them. The taller one of the two smiled and explained that they speak in any language they cared to as long as the people they were talking to wanted to become friendly; if the people didn't want to be friends the creatures would just stay in the rocks and observe. He saw the look of astonishment on the boys' faces and maybe a little disbelief. He just nodded at the boys, smiled again and gestured, inviting them to sit down.

Let's take a break...

I wanted some inspiration as at that moment in time I had no idea how the story got to this point and I certainly had no idea where it was going; I needed a few precious seconds to gather my thoughts and think fast. The boys wondered if a snack was imminent and suggested peanut butter cups and milk. I took my time, and thought a coffee might help me focus. It did.

And so the story continued...

"My name is Yowan," he said, "and my cousin is called Vajo. Welcome to our canyon, this is our home and we have been here for many, many years. It may be difficult for you to understand at first, but you see we are not human like you. We are called Pikhaupi. We were never born like you were, we simply evolve and develop, you see we are always developing and changing. We don't grow old and die like you. Time for us is very different. Vajo is the youngest among us and he is just 5 million years old, whilst I am his elder cousin, I am only 7 million; but most of the Pikhaupi are around 50 million years old and some are so old they don't even remember how old they really are."

There were gasps from the two boys. Jake asked how on earth can they survive for so long and what if they got sick and what do they eat. Josh wanted to know how often they play. Vajo joined in, smiled and told them every one thousand years they have a party and have lots of fun, and it just so happens that the party is to be that very night and would the two boys like to come? Yowan held up his hand and explained that although they were very welcome to come, they would need to understand a little more about the Pikhaupi and gestured to Vajo not to interrupt again. Yowan answered Jake's question and explained that because they are always developing, they never really get sick – there is only one disease anyway which I will explain later, all they do is just change into something slightly different. They don't eat like humans but instead they live off the limestone rocks by absorbing the many different minerals which they are made of. Vajo interrupted again to inform the boys that magnesium was his favourite treat. This time Yowan smiled and continued. "The Pikhaupi were originally formed by rain which can sometimes turn into a magic rain known as a chemical rain and this, blown by the wind, turns the limestone into the lumpy and bulging interesting shapes which they are. The Pikhaupi have no parents like human children, but they have 10 seniors who each control their own section, overseeing all erosion problems and advising when next to adjust locations. If we didn't move we would erode and disappear. It is the only disease we have and it is very rare. It's known to our people as Corroditus. It can be avoided and it's the job of the Seniors to advise us when it is time to move. We have just one million years to prepare and then we are ordered to move."

Josh asked how they moved – after all, they couldn't just walk to somewhere else, could they? Of course not, Yowan went on to explain they need to change their shapes and this takes a lot of energy so that they need to hibernate for a million years to gain enough power to do so. The last time it happened was 27 million years ago. Wow, the boys found it too much to take in at once. Josh wondered how the Pikhaupi sleep as it was obvious they didn't have any beds. This time Vajo replied describing how they all climb onto each other, and their bodies, warmed by the sun during the day, fuse together to become rock again. It didn't take very long.

The boys stared at the two Pikhaupi friends they had just made and although there were still so many questions to ask, they found that they now only wanted to play. Vajo smiled a beaming smile, showing off his enormous teeth whilst Yowan's smile showed off his strange shaped rather intricate ears. Jake thought he must have excellent hearing.

Vajo turned to his cousin and asked if the boys could now be invited to the party. Yowan thought perhaps he would need to get permission but he was unsure who he could ask because it was getting late and the fun was about to begin, so he made a decision, nodded slowly, turned towards Jake and Josh and again welcomed them to the canyon and to the Pikatoodoo, which was the Pikhaupi word for party. Vajo jumped with joy, clapped his hands and gave the boys a hug. Josh loved hugs but was a little concerned because hugging Vajo was like hugging a huge lump of playdough and he worried that he would leave his finger marks all over Vajo for ever. Yowan told the boys to hide in a small cave and wait and watch until it was time to come out and join in. Both boys tried to be as patient as possible, but it was very difficult. Neither knew what to expect and when things did start to happen it became obvious they could never have imagined what was about to take place. No one would.

What the boys saw and heard was incredible. They saw the colours of the backdrop change from cinnamons, reds, maroons and gold to a much softer pallet by the setting of the sun. Coyotes came out to play with the very rare prairie dogs. Bats flickered everywhere in the subdued light, which was now becoming tinged with pinks. In the corner under the Douglas fir trees mule deer could be seen. All the animals seemed to be dancing, whilst waiting, expectantly. A huge loud crack was heard in the distance, it was the sound of the Pikhaupi unravelling themselves one at a time, slowly at first. The children noticed that the cracking sound each disentangling Pikhaupi made was different in sound and volume from the others. Each Pikhaupi also looked so different from the others, each one unique. One was tall and so thin almost broom like, one was rather larger at the bottom tapering to a point at the top, a few had flat tops, a few had very long necks, but as they all began to disconnect themselves from each other it became clear that the sound they were making together was almost dreamlike as if the sound could be seen. The canyon was beginning to disappear and in its place was what could only be described as an array of sound, an orchestra without any instruments. It was the noise and vibrations the Pikhaupi bodies made just moving which created this amazing sound. The boys wondered if this could be the end of the Pikhaupis altogether. The ground was shaking, the noise was deafening and the boys were terrified they would disappear through Earth itself. At this stage they knew they were witnessing a once in a lifetime experience and knew only too well that this moment in time was significant. After all, it only happened every one thousand years. The orchestra of moving. Pikhaupi danced and marched, forming 10 lines. Vajo ran towards the boys and invited them to join in his line and march with them. They did their best, although it was difficult to keep up, and the dance seemed quite confusing, jumping up and down and moving in any direction all at the same time. Even so, it was great fun and it seemed that the Pikhaupis just accepted them, some even smiling at them. They can't remember how long they danced and marched with their friends or how long they played with the mule deer and climbed high in the Douglas fir trees, but they noticed a slight change in the light and both Yowan and Vajo looked a bit sad, Vajo explained that the Pikatoodoo was nearly over and all the Pikhaupi needed to return to their rock homes to rest. Both Jake and Josh said goodbye to their new friends and hugged them tight; this time Josh wasn't worried about leaving finger marks on Vajo. They thanked them and promised never ever to forget them. They watched as the canyon was slowly put back together, each Pikhaupi climbing onto each other tangling together in typical Pijhaupi style. The boys waved their goodbyes and blew kisses to them all.

Jake and Josh were both tired and they never really knew how they got back to their aunt and uncle's house. They knew that they had done though, because the next morning they awoke in their beds. It was Aunt Agatha who came in to say good morning the next day, and to apologise to the boys for not returning until later in the evening, explaining that Doris had given birth to a little girl.

The boys looked confused as they thought they were in trouble for leaving the house, but Aunt Agatha just dismissed the look as jet lag. Uncle Brian came in next and sat on Josh's bed, suggesting they make up for yesterday by taking them into the canyon for the day. Jake and Josh just looked at each other and smiled.

Aunt Agatha and Uncle Brian were quite impressed with the knowledge the boys had about the canyon and the boys spent the day trying to remember which of the rocks their friends had emerged from. They were almost beginning to think that they had dreamt the whole experience but just then they thought they saw movement at the bottom of one of the rocks...

NATIONAL RECREATIONAL AREA LAKE MEAD, LAKE MOHAVE

We were moving towards the warmer climes of California and looking forward to some gentle heat. We stopped briefly on the way at Lake Mohave some 200 or so miles from St George, a fairly easy drive, although on the way down to the lake we hit a pothole-filled dirt road.

Yet another glorious backdrop with clear blue waters of the lake. A totally manmade reservoir of the Colorado river stretching for 67 miles, its location is between the Hoover Dam and Davis Dam, the name originating from the Mohave Indians who previously inhabited the region. Interestingly, the purpose of Davis Dam was really a requirement from the 1944 Water Treaty with Mexico; its purpose is to regulate water released from the Hoover Dam for delivery to Mexico. Lake Mohave created from Davis Dam was completed in 1953 and is used for that purpose.

We spent a great 3 days here relaxing and walking, and a few energetic hours were spent on the lake in paddle boats. It was the end of November and time to think of putting together Christmas cards using the photograph taken in Utah. The boys helped in this task and by the time we left all was organised.

We spent time together planning the next few weeks in Palm Springs, including our next block of home schooling which the boys always liked to be part of. All in all, a restful time for everyone.

2009 christmas card

PALM SPRINGS, CALIFORNIA

"I must, I must, I must improve my bust, for fear for fear it slips down to my rear."

Normally my recollections of places or particular occasions come to life with music, a smell or perhaps the odd word. But, you only have to mention the words Palm Springs to me and the above ditty immediately comes into my mind. I heard those words uttered by Keith, who was repeating what he had heard minutes before. More of that later. Instead I will fast forward the journey of the two hundred and seventy two miles to reach our destination, Indio, a city close to Palm Springs, California.

Known as a desert resort city located in Riverside County in southern California's Colorado desert, Palm Springs sits comfortably within the Coachella Valley about 100 miles east of Los Angeles; it is the largest city in the county by land mass and when we visited had a population of around forty-four thousand people. The Coachella valley is surrounded by the San Bernardino, Jacinto and Santa Rosa mountains which are just breath-taking and make a stunning backdrop whichever way you look. There is lots to do here and so our stay was planned for around 6 weeks and as mentioned was taking in both Thanksgiving and Christmas. Six weeks also gave a chance to cover a lengthy home school segment and also to explore this part of California, which was an unknown to us. We carefully chose the Indian Wells RV Resort as it had a lot to offer in the form of location, and boasted three pools and hot tubs, ample clean laundry facilities, and many shower blocks, all clean and modern. It was on booking into this site that we learnt that Jake had a keen interest in American politics, in particular President Obama and his healthcare plan. An American male veteran somehow became engaged with Jake in political dialogue whilst I was doing the admin necessary when booking into a campsite. Things were taking longer than usual as our reserved site was occupied, but a lot of laughter was coming from the corner where Jake and the old man were deep in discussion. When all was done, I learnt that Jake had totally impressed his new buddy with his knowledge of the then proposed Health Care Bill and had some knowledge about diplomacy, as he was reluctant to take the democratic side, sensing that the old man veered more towards the Republicans. We checked into a temporary site for a few days before moving into our pre booked place where we would spend the rest of our stay. We got to know our Canadian neighbours and settled into a routine of home schooling in the morning and adventuring in the afternoons. My day with Josh started at seven thirty when we swam before breakfast in one of the heated pools, and could not take our eyes off the colours bouncing off the mountains surrounding the valley which were quite stunning at this time of the morning and seemed to vary each day. We liked the walk to the pool best when there had been a shower as the sight of a rainbow was just incredible nestled in with the pinks and greys of the mountain tops.

Our first adventure was to explore the local National Park which was called the Joshua Tree. It was a trip we would repeat several times during our stay as it was a round trip of sixty-odd miles taking only about 1hr and 20 minutes.

A vast eight hundred thousand acres, this park at first seemed unwelcoming and almost ruthless. Having spent some time in the Rockies in Colorado and the deserts of Arizona and Utah we all had an understanding of harsh but fragile landscapes, and we had empathy with this one. With climatic extremes this land is shaped by strong winds, sparse, spasmodic and unpredictable rainfall and very few water holes; the surroundings looked parched and maybe we could be forgiven for thinking parts of this park were dead. In fact, of course, it was all part of a delicate and fragile ecosystem that is home to both plants and animals that survive and prosper in this desert space. We looked forward to meeting the park's namesake, the Joshua tree, and it didn't disappoint. It is a prickly oddity of a tree, spiky and twisted. Being European we were quite used to olive trees with their twisted branches, but the Joshua Tree excelled and portrayed a sinister almost grotesque picture which would certainly frighten many of us if we were exposed to it in the dead of night. However, there is no accounting for taste and we grew very quickly to love these ugly trees. It was very difficult to know the age of the trees as they lack the usual growth rings found in most other trees, but we learnt that a very average life span is around one hundred and fifty years and this is gauged by height; however, there are some a lot older bearing in mind they grow about one and a half to three inches a year. Their life begins with the rare germination of a seed and its survival is thanks to the occasional rains. Birds, reptiles, mammals and insects depend on the Joshua tree for food and shelter.

Another prickly plant we discovered was the Cholla Cactus. This was one of Josh's favourite plants, maybe because it was also a bit scary and was reputed to sometimes be active. We stopped at a collection of these and walked the quarter mile loop walk which had been laid out through the plantation. The Cholla Cactus is also known as jumping cactus because the stems can very easily attach themselves to your skin if you come too close and certainly if you brush them .The stems are said to be able to jump distances, although we never found out how far and we never saw any jump; nevertheless we were careful not to go too close as we heard many stories of hikers requiring medical treatment after encountering the Cholla Cactus. The stems also get attached to many of the desert animals and as young plants grow from the stems it would account for a scattering of these plants around this enormous park.

Another day we explored the Jumbo Rocks. As the name suggests it is a collection of giant odd shaped rocks. We started this adventure by exploring Skull Rock, which was easily accessible from the roadside and the boys enjoyed the climb, especially into the eye sockets of the skull, after which we ventured towards the Jumbo rocks themselves. Here the boys spent a few hours climbing and playing amongst these massive stones.

A visit to The Lost Horse Mine was another adventure that the boys really enjoyed. The walk to the mine was about a three hour round trip over quite difficult hiking terrain and a climb of over 5,000 feet. A colourful story emerges involving gold rush legends such as cowboys, cattle rustlers, horse thieves and of course sticky-fingered miners. The mine got its name from a man called John Lang who lost a horse while driving a herd of cattle. He eventually found his horse at the camp of a cattle rustler gang called the Mahaney gang, who sent him packing and warned him not to come back. However, he later sneaked back with his father and bought the mining rights for 1000 dollars. The mine became significant in the gold rush years producing around 10,000 ounces of gold and 16,000 ounces of silver in its time from 1894 to 1931, a value today of approx. 5 million dollars. It was in 1936 that the area came under the National Park's protection; however, over time the mine crumbled and disappeared due to earthquakes and sink holes. Later work was done to preserve as much of the old mine as possible. Today the trail that leads to the mine is an adventure in itself and what's left of the mine is viewed at a distance.

As Thanksgiving was approaching we added this to the home school curriculum plus some facts fun and otherwise about California.

First of all, thanksgiving. The atmosphere around the campsite and local shops was similar to that experienced at Christmas time with an air of excitement and so not wanting to miss out we made our preparations. I made the most important decision which was the one about food. Jake helped me enormously in deciding that turkey would be the best choice, and an obvious one for the occasion, as the majority of America eats turkey on this day, apart of course from the one spared by the President. This decision was not one to be taken lightly as turkey is one of Keith's least favourite foods and Josh was not particularly enthused; however, despite this Jake and I boldly went ahead with turkey. We had to figure out how to cook this in a camp size oven but of course we solved the problem. We ended up cooking large turkey drumsticks in an American type of skillet which I can only describe as a large electric saucepan. Traditionally cooked with celery, onions and herbs then browned in the oven, we also added the English touch of roast potatoes and extra vegetables, creating turkey similar to a Christmas Day lunch. The end product was very juicy, ending Keith's thoughts and comments about dry turkey.

Thanksgiving is a quintessential American holiday, celebrated on the fourth Thursday in November; it is a family day when Americans gather to feast, parade and watch football games. As described, the traditional food is turkey roasted and American style served with mashed potato, sweet potato, stuffing, cranberry sauce, and dessert is usually pumpkin pie with ice-creams. Traditionally before the meal a prayer is given in thanks.

The origins of this day are uncertain, but possibly date back to 1621 where a feast celebrating a good harvest took place in Plymouth, Massachusetts. Another story is that a few years earlier when Pilgrims were living through a terrible drought, they decided to fast and pray for a full day of rain in July. The very next day the rain started, and in addition supplies arrived from the Netherlands into Boston harbour on board a ship which had been thought to be lost for good. A day of thanksgiving was proclaimed by Governor Bradford to offer prayers of thanks to God.

From the Texan point of view the first Thanksgiving day was in 1541 and many other States celebrated a day of prayers and thanksgiving often relating to good harvests. It was George Washington who issued the first Thanksgiving proclamation by a president of the United States on November 26th, 1789.

A day before our thanksgiving on 26th November 2009, some two hundred and twenty years later, we witnessed on national TV the President of the United States of America pardoning his first turkey after only ten months in office. President Obama officially pardoned a 45 pound Wild Turkey whose name was Courage. The President was accompanied by daughters Sasha and Malia, and after a short and meaningful speech he proclaimed that Courage was hereby pardoned and would get to spend the rest of his life in peace and tranquillity at Disneyland. I also believe he mentioned that Presidents Eisenhower and Truman actually ate their turkeys. Nevertheless, Courage was spared that terrible fate. President George H W Bush was the first President to officially pardon a turkey.

The boys' home schooling at this stop was to learn everything they could about California and these are some of the amazing fun facts they presented us with:

It is nicknamed the Golden State. Has been a state since 1850. The capital is Sacramento. The state flower is the Golden

Poppy. The state bird is the Californian Golden Quail and animal the Grizzly Bear. California is home to: the tallest waterfalls in North America – Yosemite Falls – and the lowest point in the United States, Death Valley; it is the site of America's highest known temperature – 144 degrees – and the tallest trees on Earth, redwood trees; the biggest trees on earth: giant sequoia trees. California is the US's most populous state: one in eight residents live here. The largest city is Los Angeles which has a population of 38 million (2014). The Coachella Valley is the Date Capital of the World and California grows 99.5% of all dates grown in the United States. (Arizona grows the rest.) The state produces over 17 million gallons of wine each year. It is estimated that each year there are approximately 500,000 detectable seismic tremors in California. LA laws forbid you to lick a toad. California is bigger than 85 of the smallest nations of the world. Disneyland opened in 1955; Walt Disney was afraid of mice. Until 1960 men with long hair were not allowed to enter Disneyland. Some Californian plants live a very long time –a Mojave Desert creosote bush is among the world's oldest living things at 43,000 years. The largest three-day Rodeo in the US is held on the Tehama County Fairgrounds in Red Bluff. One out of every eight music festivals in the USA are held in California. The Monterey Jazz festival in September is the oldest of its kind in the world. The Californians believe they invented the Chinese Fortune Cookie, although the Japanese in the

19th century made a similar item using sesame and miso, but without a doubt the American vanilla and butter Fortune Cookies are popular everywhere.

After this mammoth effort we felt the need to break from the usual home schooling for a day, so a vote was taken, a picnic agreed, and the Salton Sea was decided on. Just around 50 miles away and in a South East direction, located in the Sonoran Desert in Southern California. The perfect trip to have in Tobie.

The Salton Sea is one of the world's largest inland seas, approximately 45 miles long by 25 miles wide and at 227 feet below sea level it is one of the lowest spots on earth. The Salton Sea itself has a history of natural mishaps. In the early 1900s, when rainfall caused the Colorado river to swell during spring floods, water escaped the irrigation canals gushing into the ancient lake bed and by the time the flood was under control the Salton Sea was formed. Today all that water sits landlocked with only a trickle of fresh water flowing in and none going out except by evaporation. As the sea dries up, minerals become more concentrated, making the water 30% more salty than the ocean. It is a major stop for migrating birds as it lies on the Pacific flyway. Over four hundred species, many from North America, pass through between October and January so our timing was perfect.

As we sat with our picnic in the warm sunshine watching numerous birds, we realised what a much-needed break this was away from routine. Funny how we quite naturally create our routines that are necessary, but just watching these migrating birds I wondered if they ever get fed up with the same routine flying many, many miles to the same destinations year after year, or do they yearn to stay put in one place, hoping the food will last through the winter – or would perhaps boredom and depression set in? One thing for sure, Jake and Josh were having a ball getting filthy dirty, completely engrossed in some game involving noise, combat tactics and sunglasses.

After just a few days of arriving in Palm Springs, it became clear to us that this was a great location, and this helped us to fuss-free settling in and we soon relaxed. It was in the first week and a day when the home school went on longer than usual that Keith went for a walk. This was normal practice after school as all four of us needed that precious time we call space. The boys usually played games around the campsite which involved them getting dirty, I often walked into the nearest shopping mall for much needed retail therapy, and Keith would either read or take a walk. It was on his return, passing one of the pools, when he decided to check on the laundry, the laundry facilities being attached to the changing areas at the end of the pool. As he approached the gates, he heard what he later described as a soft melodic chanting. Having lived in Asia for around twenty years we were used to listening to the various incantations of the Taoists, Buddhists and often the soft early morning prayers which used to float into our bedroom each morning from the local Thai Muslim temple. Arriving from Utah armed with our recently acquired knowledge of the Mormon religion and customs, he was sensitive as well as interested in the sounds of this new chant which at first sounded almost musical. He was unable to spot the exact location of these hymn-like tunes, which was probably because his head was bowed out of respect but he soon discovered they were coming from the swimming pool. Bowing even further out of respect he realised the source was a group of about fifteen or so females of a certain age who were holding each other's hands forming a complete circle in the pool. He quickly became conscious of the fact that he couldn't turn back; in other words he had to proceed past this group and try to disappear as best he could into the laundry rooms. At this stage I think it fair to say that he must have resembled an extremely polite Japanese person or even a victim of a slipped disk, but as he was passing this spiritual group he was able to make out the exact words they were chanting.

"I must, I must,
I must improve my bust,
For fear, for fear,
It slips down to my rear."

Only in California!!

Just next door to our campsite was the Shields Date Farm. We decided one Saturday morning to pay the farm a visit and at first we couldn't figure out why Jake was so enthusiastic about visiting a date farm but as we approached on foot we soon got the gist when we noticed a huge banner advertising The Romance and Sex life of a Date which clearly was helping promote this exotic and difficult-to-grow fruit.

As we entered, we were invited to watch a short film about this intriguing farm, a family business started by Floyd and Bess Shields who came to the Californian Desert in 1924 and started the Date Garden. They were so enthusiastic about dates that they enjoyed educating their customers about Date culture. At first Mr Shields would hold lectures in the garden which eventually led to him recording his own film – the same one we watched. The film runs continuously throughout the day, lasting around fifteen minutes and is called The Romance and Sex life of a Date. We learnt that although bees and some other insects are attracted to the Date Palm pollen, the actual date production from open pollination through bees, insects and wind is often very low. Therefore, artificial pollination is used, which successfully increases production. The most common technique used in areas where labour costs are low is to cut the strands of the male flowers from a freshly opened male spathe and place 2 or 3 of the strands lengthwise in an inverted position between the strands of the female inflorescence after having already shaken some of the pollen over the female inflorescence. Where labour is expensive the procedure is mechanized. As there are few Date Farms in America it made the visit even more special and of course the Date Farm shop was quite a unique experience. We enjoyed trying all the various dates and maybe the Medjool Date was the favourite as it was perhaps the sweetest and largest, although many of the other types were good too. Here are examples. Blonde and Brunette dates. These were created by Mr Shields in 1927 by hybridizing two existing varieties. These were a medium sweet, quite dry variety. Deglet Noor date. These were lovely and sweet, almost nutty, good for snacking and baking. Abbada Date, a black date, quite dry with a strong flavour, not one of my favourites. Barhi Date, very sweet, tasted by Josh but not recommended. Honey Date, this date had Jake's approval as it was soft and a bit creamy. Thoory Date seemed a bit dry and chewy. Zahide date, a semi-dry date and not too sweet. The shop sold a huge date milkshake which was delicious and we all enjoyed it. We left having spent, as one does, a small fortune on dates, and many nut butters. What impressed me was the lack of any chemical fertilizers or pesticides and everything used in production was natural. We were told that Shields Date Farm was the inventor of Date Sugar sold as an alternative to the heavily refined cane sugar, delicious.

During our American trip Josh lost a few of his milk teeth and the tooth fairy was ever present. We also noticed that he was growing a new tooth over one of his old teeth thus producing a double tooth, and having no past experience of this we thought a visit to the dentist was in order. It was after this dental visit that Josh decided dentists were OK after all, as he was told that his double tooth was OK and the old tooth would fall out naturally and also, because he had no cavities, he was entitled to a toy. This was apparently company policy. It took the receptionist about 15 minutes to find a toy as these were obviously rarely needed and I think she secretly sneaked out to buy one from the close-by Walmart! Anyhow, Josh was delighted and we were relieved that no further dental work was required.

California boasts of a wonderful and very varied climate, one where you can breakfast in sunshine and dine amongst snowy mountains. So on Christmas Eve we decided to have some fun on top of the San Jacinto mountain peak. We set off after breakfast in the sun and, equipped with warm sweaters and anoraks, we drove for around 40 minutes to the base of the Aerial Tram, which climbs up the mountain. We bought tickets and boarded the largest rotating aerial tram in the world. So from the floor of the Coachella valley to near the top of San Jacinto peak we travelled. The tram is surprisingly large with a Tardis effect inside, it carries a maximum of eighty passengers, it makes two complete revolutions on the journey that takes about twelve minutes. We could see California's Salton Sea to the east, which was around 75 miles away, and we were told looking north on a clear day one could see as far as Las Vegas in Nevada, about 200 miles away. We arrived at the top some 8500 feet above sea level and many degrees colder and we donned our jumpers and coats. We learned later that the air was 40 degrees cooler compared to the warm air we had left behind in the Sonoran Desert. The first port of call was the purchasing of snow boards. We were going snowboarding! The boys got straight down to learning the art of snowboarding and very naturally and easily acquired this skill, and considering this was only the second time in their lives that they had seen snow we were very impressed. Next up were Mum and Dad who didn't fare so well. Much less refined, we took out the odd tree on the way down, spinning off in the wrong direction which amused a few people, mainly children; however, we did not give up. When we had enough it was our job to build the biggest snowman possible, the boys pitched in and we were somewhat better at this, although I have seen less ugly snowmen, but we all did well especially as the two adults were without gloves. Such an enjoyable trip and one that was repeated. On our final trip the boys, knowing this was the last time they would encounter snow on this American trip, decided to cash in their snow boards and sold them half price to a brother and sister who were delighted with their bargains. So, winners all round.

I can't leave this chapter without mentioning Tobie (bless her). Having noticed she had developed a natural fresh air conditioning system through holes in the soft top hood, which were gradually becoming bigger on every trip, I thought it was about time I tactfully mentioned this to Keith and the boys. On examination, it was clear the soft top was in great need of repair – there were many torn places and weak points, particularly around the roll bar and wind shield. We all agreed it needed to be replaced. We received a few quotes from the local garages and decided their prices were very expensive as they were charging so much for the labour. After some research we decided to buy direct from the internet and assemble a new soft top ourselves, saving around $500 US. It seemed to make sense, but I couldn't shake off the memory of the three hours it took us to assemble a wooden clothes horse from Ikea. Anyhow, we went ahead and ordered and in no time at all a big box arrived containing the canvas top and instructions. It did seem confusing but common sense and perseverance got us through, and Keith really did excel. Yes, it took longer than it should, but we now had a brand new top for our jeep.

Double header

30th JANUARY 2010

AS you Can see I AM I Am

Very out of date, bet me see if I

CAn remember what has happened;

Chrismas was wonderful, SANTA

bought me 2 clone wars fiures

And one was clone commanper copy.

NANA boughts me A book About

Michael JAckson. I ALso gotA

ripstick And A spider droid.

The cAmp site was Lovely, it

hAd 3 swiming pools And very

nice Showhers.

Jake's Xmas diary

California

PalmSpring

Cholla cactus

I went to Joshua tree N.p. and I saw the cholla cactus. The cholla cactus is spicke. Another name is the jumping cactus.

Joshiescholla cactus diary

Joshua Tree

SAN DIEGO

I awoke early today which I suppose is my norm and busied myself getting ready for the journey ahead from Palm Springs to San Diego. It's quite a typical start really, organising breakfasts and the general customary preparations inside the coach before moving on to our next destination.

At this stage who would know that today would be the day I would singlehandedly be responsible for reducing two very healthy rubber Jeep tyres to what I can only describe as two hot smoking, round, bald canvas rings. I must admit that it was very easy. It just took a moment, a mere twist of the fingers, surely it could happen to anyone…

We left Palm Springs in the morning after doing the usual outside safety checks to the coach and Tobie, double checking that nothing was left behind and everything was in the right place. It was always my responsibility and one I enjoyed doing, a pleasant routine. We both knew the first part of the journey would be a bit tricky and Keith was a bit nervous, but he really excelled in the handling of the coach and was in total control of the numerous hairpin bends which seemed to go on forever. We did notice, however, that a few overtaking cars waved to us but we just waved back to these friendly American drivers. It was when we reached the turnpike (an American title I picked up meaning motorway) another driver in an overtaking car was pointing to our Jeep using more aggressive body language pointing behind to the Jeep. It was at this moment that time stood still and slow motion took over. First my breathing was slow, calm even, as it was taking in the full aroma of burning rubber and then I had the flashback. Very slowly I put my hand in my pocket and found the Jeep keys. These should have been in the ignition and half turned, so that the front wheels would not lock. I had locked them in place when doing the morning routine checks and they had been dragged sideways for 50 miles. (I find it amusing looking back that I could clearly see myself doing the deed, but at the time it just didn't register). There is not too much more to mention on this subject except of course that I was not very popular, causing my husband to use language I have never heard him use before. Two new front tyres cost 600 dollars.

We had booked a week at the Mission Bay campsite and arrived a bit subdued after the day's troubles and our mood didn't improve much when we discovered the campsite facilities were not up to scratch, despite the location being superb. The evening walk around the bay improved all our moods and that evening we made plans for the next few weeks. Firstly, we needed to find another campsite after our booked seven days expired and hopefully one close by. Next, we promised to find Josh a two-wheeler bike without stabilisers and Jake a Rip-stick. We also made plans to visit Sea World, the Maritime Museum, Lego Land and much more.

Whilst we were staying at the Mission Bay site, we decided to take a seven-day break in the home schooling and just enjoy our surroundings. We managed to find a suitable bike for Josh at Costco as well as a rip-stick for Jake and both were to prove quite a challenge. After many attempts and tumbles, Josh mastered the two-wheeler and ended up riding like a pro and as there were many safe places to ride, practising was easy. On New Year's Eve Josh lost his second baby tooth.

Jake also mastered the rip-stick although he found this very frustrating at times as it manoeuvred in a different way to a skateboard, having only two offset wheels and is self-propelled with alternating movement of the legs and feet. His balance was good though, which helped him a lot.

Josh and I soon got into an early morning and early evening walking routine which always took in the Bay and we soon forgot about the lack of good facilities at the camp.

A lot of walking was also involved when we investigated the Maritime Museum located in downtown San Diego. It was a great day exploring all the historic vessels that had been skilfully restored and maintained, and exploring the great age of sail and steam. I think our favourite must be the Star of India, the world's oldest active metal sailing ship which started her life at Ramsey Shipyard in the Isle of Man in 1863, built of iron for the Indian jute trade. She was known as Euterpe (the muse of music) ,a fully rigged windjammer ship built to carry cargo for long distances in the 19th and 20th century. She had several owners in her time, one of whom required the ship to carry passengers to New Zealand. It wasn't until 1902 that she became known as the Star of India and after being re-rigged she began carrying fishermen, cannery workers, coal, and canning supplies from Oakland to Nushagak in the Bering Sea (North Pacific Ocean), returning with holds of canned salmon. In 1957 restoration began and in 1976 the Star of India was put to sea again; she houses exhibits for the Maritime Museum.

Another vessel we spent time on was The Berkeley, a steam ferryboat that was built in 1898 and operated for 60 years in San Francisco Bay. Now quite at home at the Maritime Museum housing the museum's offices, a major research library, workshop, model shop, the museum store, and a special events venue playing host to thousands of weddings.

Next we investigated a Soviet Navy Submarine B-39, which was commissioned in the early 1970s and served on active duty for more than 20 years. Three hundred feet in length and displacing more than 2000 tons, the B-39 is among the largest conventionally powered submarines ever built. She was designed to track US and NATO warships throughout the world's oceans. The B-39 stalked many of the US Navy ships home ported in San Diego. This all ended after the collapse of the Berlin Wall, which signalled the eventual termination of the Cold War. The submarine carried a crew of 78 and we found it hard to imagine them living in such cramped conditions. She was classed as low tech but lethal as she carried 24 torpedoes. I for one was glad when our tour ended, and we could breathe in fresh air once again.

We next visited the USS Midway aircraft carrier, now a museum. It was the longest serving US carrier, being in action from 1945 to 1992 and over 200,000 sailors sailed on her during that time. There is a collection of different retired aircraft on the deck, most of them built in California. It is a massive vessel with multiple decks and corridors, so it was no surprise that we lost the boys. Fortunately, we knew they couldn't get off the vessel without us and we eventually found them running around the huge flight deck having great fun. A good if not tiring day which we concluded by finding ice-creams in the clean and vibrant city of San Diego.

It was time we learnt a few facts about San Diego:

It is situated on the Pacific coast in Southern California, 120 miles south of LA, sharing a 15-mile border with Mexico and covers an area of 372 square miles. Historically home to the Kumeyaay people, it was first visited by the European explorer Juan Rodriguez Cabrillo who claimed to have discovered San Diego Bay in 1542 (200 years before the first

Europeans actually settled in the area). San Diego is known for its great climate, natural deep-water harbour and its long association with the US Navy. It now hosts the largest naval fleet in the world. Other interesting but not very useful one-liners about San Diego:

- Fallbook in San Diego is the avocado capital of the world.
- WD 40 was invented in San Diego in 1953.
- Hypnotism is banned in public schools.
- None of the man-made lakes in San Diego allow swimming.

Charles Lindbergh flew from San Diego on May 9th, 1927 in the Spirit of St Louis, headed for New York and then non-stop to Paris.

Our second campsite in San Diego was Chula Vista. This was located about 16 miles away from Mission Bay, about a twenty-minute drive. This site was great, overlooking the Marina and Bayside Park, complete with pool and gym. All facilities were of good quality. There was plenty of space around each plot, offering much privacy complete with picnic tables and chairs. We planned to stay 4 weeks at this site. It was here that Jake and Josh met their friends Gabe and David, who became soulmates for the rest of our stay, and as we were hitting a period of intense home schooling it was good for them to play out and cycle together.

Throughout our American trip we were often reminded

that our English language, the language we share with our American counterparts, can be very different. When we first arrived at our new campsite we suggested to the boys that they cycle around the campsite keeping to the pavements as the roads were busy with arriving RVs. This was a bad idea as the onsite Janitor had rules of his own. He came looking for us, complaining that he had told our boys three times to get off the sidewalk and they just ignored him. They, of course, hadn't a clue what a sidewalk was and continued riding. As soon as the Janitor realised we were British, he nodded knowingly and walked away, shaking his head, mumbling something about learning proper English.

Chula Vista was a great site set within the marina and this time the facilities were very good with pool, gym, clubrooms and many clean bathrooms. There were several good restaurants, and a good live music bar; it was on our first night we caught up with the boys dancing to an Eric Clapton song along with other grown up groupies. Which reminds me, it was my sister's birthday and it was great talking to her at that age when life begins!

We began some intense home schooling which both boys seemed quite happy with. The schooling itself was supposed to be from 9.00 to 12.30 but often we found it naturally extended beyond 12.30, in particular with Jake who was always happy to finish his essay or reading or research. Josh seemed to enjoy reading, getting through many books.

We enjoyed a day out at Lego Land which suited Josh very well as this theme park with aquarium was younger child orientated, set in around 128 acres with many rides including 3 water rides. Josh loved the dinosaur explorer island, digging for fossils and other treasures in a large sand area helped along by his older brother. They both enjoyed the police and fire academy where they took part in an exercise involving putting out a simulated building fire and returning to their truck as fast as possible.

Lego is one of those toys which really doesn't seem to age. I know both boys play for hours with it, but it can be annoying for parents who are constantly finding Lego pieces under beds, hidden in carpet pile, even in kitchen cupboards and often in the hoover. It is a Danish invention, the name itself being an abbreviation of "Leg godt" meaning play well. Founded in 1932, it is still a family business growing from a small carpenter's workshop to a modern day global enterprise which is now one of the world's largest manufacturer of toys. Who would have thought a simple interlocking brick system with unlimited building possibilities would capture children's imaginations worldwide.

We had another great day out when we visited Sea World. There is something very relaxing when surrounded by fish, so as well as having a fun day it also had a calming effect on us all.

We were able to get up close to many of the sea creatures

and were able to touch the smaller tide pool creatures such as star fish and even some of the sea urchins. The larger fish like the Sting Rays were the most popular with the boys, as they were able to touch the wings of the fish as they flew past. The penguins and sea lions were also a hit. The turtle reef also proved to be popular with us all. Here we viewed loggerhead, hawksbill and green sea turtles, some of which were over fifty years old.

Of course, with anything to do with a water park come water rides, none of which disappointed. We started with the Shipwreck Rapids, in which a slow winding river turns into rolling white water rapids, which in turn prepares you for the grand waterfall finale. Another water thrill was the Riptide Rescue, which starts out in a large sea turtle vessel constantly spinning, taking many turns on its way and soaking us all. The last thrill we encountered was the Wild Arctic simulator, an exciting experience full of adventure from a jet helicopter and taking in perilous icy landscapes of the Arctic Circle, manoeuvring through treacherous icy peaks and valleys en route to Base Station Wild Arctic.

We were coming to the end of our stay in San Diego; however, being so close to the Mexican border we couldn't resist making a trip into another country. We decided to cross the border into Tijuana and make our way to Rosarito beach. The next chapter describes this visit.

TIJUANA, MEXICO

I t was going to be a side order and one we discussed together
as a family to decide if it was worth doing. We decided it
was – after all, San Ysidro, the Mexican border area in San
Diego, was only 20 miles away, so, how could we not go? The
questions Keith and I asked ourselves were, is it safe? and how
complicated is the paperwork? We decided the paperwork for
us, with our 6-month visas, was straightforward and for three
days if we kept to the tourist areas everything should be good.

Home schooling for a few days leading up to a Mexican visit
was of course all about Mexico. The flag was straightforward
for the boys to copy with colours of green, white and red with
a central coat of arms of an eagle, a cactus and a serpent. The
plan was to visit Tijuana, which is just across the border, a
border crossing which is one of the busiest in the world with
over 30 million people crossing in a year.

Tijuana is steeped in history, from being home to the
Kumeyaay tribe to the arrival of Europeans and missions to

the American civil war in 1846-1848. Mexico, having gained independence from Spain some twenty odd years earlier, fought the United States as an independent country and unfortunately for the Mexicans suffered defeat. This downfall resulted in the loss of almost a third of its territory causing the loss of modern-day Arizona, New Mexico, Utah, Nevada, and most of California. Texas became independent from Mexico earlier in 1836 and briefly became a sovereign state.

The modern-day Tijuana is a busy city of some 246 square miles with a population of around 1.3 million. It is famous for its bars, restaurants, shops and beaches where local Americans go for some home-grown Mexican culture as well as authentic Margaritas and Tequilas. We also discovered that Tijuana assembles more televisions than almost any other city in the world, as well making more than three quarters of digital thermometers worldwide, or so we were told.

It took us just 45 minutes to arrive at the border area of San Ysidro, we secured a parking space after a while and hoped Tobie would be safe, although when we looked back at our Jeep we were pretty certain nobody would be interested in taking it for a joyride. As we walked through to the border we sauntered through some shops where we bought the boys jackets, which of course they insisted on wearing immediately. We also tasted our first Mexican coffee which was surprisingly mild.

It was very easy crossing the border into Mexico although

we did notice the very long queues going the other way and took note to leave in good time for the return journey. We took a bus from the border to the bustling town of Tijuana, the main drag being a street called Avenida Revolution which was crowded, very touristy and noisy, full of the usual bars, restaurants and shops. Bienvenido a Mexico. Did it remind us a little of Manila, maybe not quite so much poverty? After asking a few people where we could locate the bus that would take us to Rosarito, we eventually boarded and drove out to the beach area heading toward The Rosarito Beach Hotel. When the bus stopped at a hopeful place we alighted and soon realised it was the wrong stop and started walking in a direction we thought was correct, as you do. Luckily we travelled light, so a 20 minute walk wasn't too bad. The hotel was OK and right on the beach, and I guess worth the walk.

It was such a relaxing three days as the boys were more than content to mess around on the beach making sand dens and collecting the most enormous shells. It always amazed us how children are just so contented with a beach and sea. Occasionally Mum and Dad would chip in and help with the tunnel or the moat or even a mountain range. We walked miles in all directions on the beach; we did investigate the local town, purchased a few souvenirs in the shape of a martini glass and a few shot glasses which were taller and slimmer than usual. In the evening we sampled tequilas in the hotel bar.

With regards to tequila, this drink is the most famous and popular in Mexico, hence it's the national drink. Therefore it was only right to give it the time and justice the drink deserved. It took us the three nights we were in Mexico and visits to the local souvenir shops who all sold an array of different types of Tequila, along with visiting a few liquor shops who sold a vast assortment of tequila shot glasses to fully understand and do justice to Tequila. It is also fair to admit that neither Keith or myself particularly liked the drink much. It was mainly at parties and leaving dos where we had experienced the ritual of salt on the back of the hand or at the crease of the elbow, a shot of clear tequila swallowed in one go followed by sucking on a wedge of lime. Frankly the process didn't do much for me, especially the hangover the next day. But here in Mexico we were learning. First, and something neither of us knew, before, Tequila is made by distilling the juice from the blue Agave plant. The plants themselves take eight years to mature and the core is used in the distilling. There are many types of tequila but simply put they fall into three main types. Bianco, this is the white liquid which is most popular in bars outside Mexico and is considered by Mexicans as rough, Reposado which is rested and aged between two to twelve months, and Aiiejo meaning vintage and aged between one and three years. Aiiejo is drunk at room temperature. Like whiskeys, tequila improves with age and becomes more mellow to taste and amber in colour. Although most are never aged for too long. The type the Mexicans drink mainly is Aiiejo or extra Aiijo which is sipped and not taken as a shot. We realised the mature Tequilas were quite good and didn't really need the salt and lime routine although we did notice one or two locals were sucking on the lime dipped in salt as they finished their drink. The barman in the hotel warned us never to drink Tequila that is less than 100% blue agave and never drink with sugar.

As we were packing to leave, we noticed the boys' rucksacks were very heavy and it turned out that they had included as many enormous shells as would fit in. It was a decision they eventually agreed to, but clearly they were not happy with having to return most of them to the beach. Although when we did arrive back at the coach the number of shells seemed to have multiplied somewhat.

We gave ourselves some extra time returning to the border and we needed it. The queues were very long and very slow due to very tight border security, which was heavily patrolled – the USA trying to prevent illegal immigration and of course smuggling. The immigration officer made it clear to us that we did not have the correct documentation to re-enter the United States, but we made it clear to the immigration officer that we did. Mistake, you do not argue with these officers. We were told to join another long queue only to find out we had the correct documents in the first place. A typical story. Nevertheless, we thoroughly enjoyed our trip to Mexico.

TERLINGUA, TEXAS

A few years ago we had enjoyed a holiday in Colorado staying in a wonderful log cabin high in the Rocky Mountains. It was a great place for many reasons. One was an abundance of bikers all "of a certain age". The long flowing grey hair coupled with the various soft floral printed shirts reflected a long-gone era from the Hippie period. Most of these exotics were riding the most amazing machines, almost all of them beautifully cared for Harley-Davidsons. There were so many of them gathering together at certain times of the day at various venues from main road to rough terrain that it conjured up a realisation that these vibrant characters were the modern-day cowboys. It was not until we arrived at a place called Terlingua in Texas that this concept of the modern cowboy was reconsidered.

It took us three days to arrive at our next destination which was Big Bend National Park. Our route took us through Arizona where we stayed at a campsite called Dateland, which was very basic but good for the boys as it seemed to have large areas where they could grub safely to their hearts' content. The next evening found us in New Mexico at a place called Deming and a campsite with the charming name of Dream Catcher. Here we felt like time had stopped in the 1950s with the large boxy furniture and a dress code which seemed to consist of waisted button through dresses for the women and lambswool pullovers for the men. Our next night was spent in Texas at Van Horne. Unfortunately, Josh had a high temperature, the first casualty since we started out, but luckily it cleared up quickly. The journey from San Diego had taken us through some stunning countryside but being so close to Mexico we were stopped by the Border Control Police on several occasions and interrogated and our documents examined. However, we always managed to convince them that we were not harbouring any illegal people or contraband and, after showing the necessary documents and answering the many questions they left us to get on with our journey. However, we experienced that same old uneasy feeling we would never get used to when armed police entered our home.

With three days on the road it seemed a good opportunity to consider our next location or locations with the boys. The main topic being the great river The Rio Grande, or Rio Bravo as the Mexicans call it. Like most children our boys' interests were quite eclectic, their enthusiasms moving from Star Wars to Cowboys at the drop of a hat. Therefore to get into the drama of where we were going we visited the 1950s and the most famous cowboy of them all, John Wayne, playing a cavalry officer who must deal with the most murderous villains of all time, the Apaches. We all thought that the Apaches made the most colourful and intriguing Baddies. The film we talked about was of course "The Rio Grande". Another famous film we discussed was "Rio Bravo" filmed later in the 50s also starring John Wayne, plus Dean Martin, Ricky Nelson and rather surprisingly, I thought, Angie Dickinson, who was then 27. We discovered later, however, that many of the cowboy films relating to The Rio Grande were actually filmed in Utah and Arizona.

The river itself is the fifth longest in the United States and among the top twenty in the world, extending from the San Juan Mountains of Colorado to the Gulf of Mexico some nineteen hundred miles further on, and it forms most importantly a one thousand two hundred and fifty mile segment of border between the US and Mexico. It passes from Colorado through the San Luis Valley into New Mexico through Albuquerque and Las Cruces to El Paso, Texas on the Mexican border. Use of the river water is regulated by The Rio Grande Compact, an interstate pact between Colorado, New Mexico and Texas; and in addition a treaty between the United States and Mexico. The river itself is over appropriated as there are more users for the water than there is water in the river, a concern to most farmers as they rely on this water for their crops.

Over the years the Rio Grande has been explored by many people including the Pueblo Indians who named it Posoge (big river). Many Spanish explorers travelled along the river and later French explorers tried to claim the river as part of Louisiana. In 1928 Mexico abolished slavery, and it was at this time that numerous slaves from Texas began to flee across the Rio Grande in search of their freedom in Mexico. It wasn't until much later when the flow of freedom seekers reversed, and today it is the Mexicans seeking a better way of life in the United States who now attempt to cross the Rio Grande into America.

We arrived at The Big Bend RV Park early evening and were blown over by the mountain sunset, which was an array of vibrant hues ranging from yellow to orange and which later became richer in colour enhancing the surrounding mountain backdrop. Simply stunning. Over dinner we made plans for the following few days and couldn't wait to start investigating.

First we headed along the river towards a town called Presidio, taking our time, stopping many times on the way to take photos, and generally breathing in the atmosphere whilst passing through what seemed to be ghost towns. It was on one of these stops in a very small-town petrol station that our previous thoughts of the modern-day cowboy with the grey haired pony tail flowing in the wind, wearing the flowered shirt and perched on top of a gleaming growling

Harley was quite wrong, because clearly here in this small-town petrol station we were looking at least half a dozen local real deal cowboys. There were six or seven of these charismatic characters all oozing individuality. These guys were not to be confused or mistaken for eccentrics or oddballs, these guys fitted very comfortably into the context of their surroundings. Not sure if it was the Stetsons, or the cravats, or the traditional Levi Strauss jeans complete with the conch large buckled belts coupled with the yolk embroidered shirts under a leather "weskit" that held my total fascination, or if it was the footwear. I think it must have been the latter because something stirred my memory. I had seen this type of footwear before, improbable as it may sound. It too had looked to be perfectly at home in its local habitat. I had seen ranges of cowboy boots made from leathers varying from cowhide, snake, ostrich, alligator, lizard, elk and buffalo, in styles with calf designs and squared off "Roper" style heels. Shaped into the boot were ornate appliques with decorative stitching. There were Cuban heels and two tone pointed toes. As odd as it might sound, the place I'm referring to having seen these before is of course La Forret in the Harajuku area in Tokyo, where everything totally off the wall can be discovered. The one thing the Tokyo footwear didn't offer, which our real-life cowboys did, was that the cowboys boots all had sliver spurs attached to them, jangling as they walked and bringing back the John Wayne images again. I have no doubt these spurs made their Dodge Ram trucks go faster and herd cattle better, but to us it cemented the fact that we were in cowboy country. As we left the petrol station we got a kick when they tipped their Stetsons and waved us goodbye. These were the real cowboys, modern, clean and stylish.

We travelled further along the river valley, enjoying the desert roller-coaster ride until the road reached right to the river's edge where we took a break to walk around. There were a few security police and border control agents patrolling the area and there were notices everywhere informing us that accepting any form of anything which had come from across the Mexican side of the river was classed as contraband and it would be a federal offence. All this to us at first seemed a bit over the top, but we needed to understand the history and politics behind the two countries and the river. As we walked further on we passed on our side of the river a few trinkets perched on the bank enticing tourists to purchase. There were no fixed prices, it was just left up to the tourist to donate. These small gifts were a mixture of tiny homemade straw dolls, tin pendants, attractive stones, a few shells; it seemed as if small children had made and collected these in a school project kindergarten class. As we walked on past these precious knick-knacks we got the feeling we were being watched. Being as subtle as we could we kept glancing over our shoulders, our eyes wandering to the Mexican side of the river. There we could see slight movements and light reflections in the desert cactus, grasses and plants. We imagined eyes watching us and at the time it certainly felt surreal. As we wandered further on, we discovered a hot spring pool with more trinkets dotted around the area. We decided to get some therapeutic relief by sitting and dangling our feet in the warm rock pool. We seemed to be there for ages, but it had relaxed us and had put a spring back in our step. This is when we again noticed a few armed security police patrolling up and down the river bank constantly watching the Mexican side with what looked like expensive high-grade binoculars. At one point we could see the police directing their gazes at us through their lenses. They were watching to see if we were going to leave money and take one of the trinkets on offer, which would mean we would be in possession of illegal contraband. They would then hope to catch the Mexican who was brave enough to swim across the river to collect the money. It was tempting to do this as we were familiar with the poverty levels in Mexico, but we didn't really want to run the risk of being in possession of contraband and being detained by any law enforcement agency, so we surreptitiously left a donation, nevertheless trying to hide it where the watching Mexican could see but the American police could not. We think we were successful, but surely a far cry from the real problem, the drug cartels.

We left the river side heading back in the direction of the campsite and decided to stop and explore the ghost town of Terlingua. It was a small strip of buildings consisting of a general store, a couple of artist shops – understandable as the light is so good here – a café, one tourist shop, a gas station, a few bars and a restaurant which used to be a theatre. We found some unusual gift items in the General Store and were fascinated with the sales assistant who was only too happy to tell all sorts of tales about the area and its people. Firstly, the lady explained that when you get a job in Terlingua you keep it. She herself had worked at the shop as a young girl, impressed the owner, left for the bright lights of Houston and returned many years later, asked for her job back and got it. Luckily for us it was a quiet time in the shop and she told us more about the area.

It was once a mining town back in the mid-1880s when the discovery of cinnabar was made. The liquid metal mercury is extracted from cinnabar. This discovery generated work and brought miners to the area, creating a thriving city of 2,000 people. The cinnabar ran out and now the only remnants of the old days are the ghost towns and several capped and abandoned cinnabar mines. Nowadays Terlingua is known to attract drifters and dropouts who fit in perfectly with the remaining locals, although this may take a little time. Friday and Saturday night visits to the famous bar La Kiva and drinking with the locals helped newcomers to integrate. La Kiva was known throughout the area mainly because of a potent cocktail named "The Mind Eraser", which is made up of several ingredients including substantial portions of vodka and Kahlua topped with club soda and drunk through a straw. There are many tales of drunken brawls which would ensure that newcomers and locals remained firm friends forever.

Apart from the Rio Grande, Terlingua is not on the way to anywhere. There are few TVs, and the cell phone signals are often too weak to get any signal at all. The nearest main shopping mall is about 250 miles away. The local attractions include the hot dry afternoon in summer, tarantulas, scorpions, camel spiders, rattlesnakes, abandoned mine shafts and poverty. Notwithstanding all this, the area has a certain fascination. The locals welcome tourism as it is the largest money maker. Visitors come to the National Park, to canoe the Rio Grande, to hike the mountains, or just to chill, drink and gaze at stars at night. As a result the population consists of artists, park rangers, retirees with old RVs, mountain bikers, old Vietnam vets, river guides and sales assistants like our friendly lady who went on to say that the population of the whole area is only a hundred or so. They don't take to government employees much and don't agree with the latest census figures showing a population of 58. Everyone knows the story of the government worker bitten by a pet Javelina whilst trying to collect census data and who then left the area immediately. (A Javelina is a kind of hoofed mammal resembling a type of wild pig.)

Terlingua's reputation is very much of outlaw country, but we were assured the residents are protective of their homes and each other. We could have gone on listening to her for hours, but she suddenly announced she had to leave and in seconds she was gone. When we looked around we saw that there was nobody left in charge of the shop. Not long afterwards half a dozen or more cowboy types came in and raided the beer fridge. The system for payment was simple: they wrote their name on a slate and put a tick by their name, denoting how many beers they had taken. Trust!

On our way out of the shop we noticed a crowd gathering on the porch outside the restaurant and some musicians gathering. A young lady playing the violin, and older lady with a guitar, an elderly man with some type of harmonica and a cowboy type playing a wash board. The night's entertainment had begun and not a TV or phone in sight. As we headed back to our jeep to return to the campsite, we noticed a sign that made both Keith and I shudder. It was a metal square sign with a picture of a gun and the words "in this town we don't call 911". Next to it was a battered old truck with a window sticker. "Don't need no car alarm I got a Smith and Wesson." Scary!

The next day we headed off to the Big Bend National Park. As we entered the park and wound our way up to the visitors' lodge, we noticed a line of rather large dustbins. Each bin was tightly closed and each bin had the same warning sign advising all visitors to ensure all bins were securely shut after use to avoid the wild brown bears tipping the bins over to rummage for an instant meal. This set the scene for our visit. The boys were on bear watch. The visitors' lodge was an excellent starting place for information, as not only were the staff very helpful and well informed, there were many leaflets to pick up or books to buy and, as in most of the national parks, there was a short and very informative film to watch. We discovered that there are over 1200 species of plant, over 450 species of bird, 56 species of reptile and 75 mammals in the Park. In addition, there are many geological features from ancient history such as sea fossils and dinosaur bones. Big Bend covers over 800,000 acres and for over 1000 miles, the Rio Grande/ Rio Bravo creates the border between the two countries. The park was simply named after a stretch of about 100 miles of Rio Grande which forms a large bend in the river at the Texas-Mexico border.

As we drove through the park the boys were eagerly looking out for bears, although thankfully not successfully. We noticed the desert change into the more mountainous terrain of the Chiso Mountains with various evergreen and oak trees. This park was fascinating whether it was for the bears, or the environment itself as it merged from desert to mountains, or just the diversity of plants and animals. It certainly held a captive audience. That night we became stargazers as we stared up at the thousands of stars and bright planets in the very clear night sky. A suitable ending to a most enjoyable visit.

Beginning to gather on the porch

Rio Grande river Mexico on the left

MUSTANG ISLAND, TEXAS

It was going to be a fairly long drive to Mustang Island, some 560 miles from Big Bend National Park, so we decided on a more relaxed pace and planned to break the journey, heading for Del Rio for the night. We were getting used to the border police making their routine checks every time we ran parallel to the Mexican border but still there was a resentment to guns being brought inside our home when these checks were being carried out – after all, guns are killing machines. We noticed that there were a couple of police vehicles driving along an empty path with tyres attached to the rear of their cars smoothing the ground, apparently for quick border chases. Our next campsite was full of character, a good choice featuring a lot of wood, most of which had been reused from an old Texas Ranch. We could be forgiven for thinking we had walked into a cowboy filmset, maybe with John Wayne again? It only seemed fitting that a Texan steak should be the meal that evening which we all enjoyed. The next day was an early rise as we were all eager to move on, but, on doing the usual routine vehicle checks, a large nail was found attached to the front tyre causing air to slowly leak out, therefore a replacement had to be found. This took some time but we were on our way by noon, with a new tyre fitted and some $680 lighter. Good job we had insurance.

It took us another night stopover until we reached Mustang Island, having driven through constant rain. We noticed the temperature had dropped quite a bit. We checked into the Gulf Water RV site, Port Aransas, and it didn't disappoint, with miles and miles of sandy beach dunes to the back of us framing the Gulf of Mexico. As far as home schooling was concerned, we were ahead of ourselves, so a little revision everyday on the basics was all that was needed, and the rest of the time the boys spent on their projects. Jake was really into the Indian tribes but there were just so many of them. At the same time he was working on his other project, which he called his Business, whilst Josh was concentrating on his diary. This meant there was plenty of time to investigate and really enjoy. We spent a lot of time on the beach, enjoying walks amongst the sand dunes, the boys having fully developed imaginations became pirates, Indians, FBI agents and even the two musketeers on a regular basis. The bird life was quite incredible, including egrets, pelicans and cranes, even including blue ones, although we still debate if we actually saw the rare giant blue crane.

Mustang Island is a barrier island on the Texan coast; it stretches for 18 miles from Corpus Christi to Port Aransas, the JFK causeway connecting it to Corpus Christi. To the south is Padre Island, which is the largest of the Texan barrier islands, boasting a length of 113 miles. The only town on Mustang Island is Port Aransas and Jake helped us with the history. Originally inhabited by the Karankawa Indians who took up residence from Galveston Bay to Corpus Christi Bay. The Karankawa Indians led a nomadic existence, migrating from the mainland to the coast. The most popular area was a small fishing village known as Sand Point on what Europeans called Wild Horse Island, later known as Mustang Island. Later on, around the 19th century, Port Aransas was known for the many pirates who arrived all searching for riches of some kind. A famous captain named Capt John La Fitte and his buccaneers spent time exploring the Texan coast and settled on Port Aransas as the place to make their camp. According to legend and the many rumours surrounding Port Aransas, there are many treasures buried beneath it. The boys, of course, were delighted with this idea but were not quite sure how to go about looking for such treasures.

We walked regularly into the Old Town as it never disappointed. The old fishing village lives on in the eastern part with its sugary pastel painted wooden houses and shops.

It reminded us of Key West but maybe these colours were slightly stronger. Here you had many interesting shops and houses mixed in with artist studios and specialist food stores mainly selling their fresh catches of fish and seafood. Overall it was a lively town. Jake and I often used to walk to one of the many fish outlets to buy our evening meal, often quite a large assortment ranging from catfish, prawns, squid, mussels and scallops, which he managed to persuade me to buy. Always a popular meal, especially for me as seafood this fresh requires very little cooking and very simple ingredients, butter, salt, herbs and lemon. It became known as a medley of fish as named by Jake and even to this day is still a favourite.

As the weekend approached, we made plans to visit Corpus Christi on Sunday which happened to be Valentine's Day and thought Sunday lunch would be a good idea. Using the car ferry, we picked our time as the timetable was limited, running between 2 and 6 ferries a day but it did run 7 days a week and it was free of charge. It connected Mustang Island at Port Aransas to the mainland via the Aransas Pass. What we didn't expect to see on the 10-minute ferry journey were dolphins keeping us company in the Corpus Christi Channel, along with many seagulls and pelicans. It was Josh who advised us all that the dolphins were the bottlenose variety. They seemed to be oblivious to the large ships and tugs around them and just concentrated on pleasing the passengers as they seemed to jump in sequence. Such a good journey and when we arrived and found parking at Corpus Christi, Josh went off on his bike along the boulevard whilst Jake rip-sticked not far behind. It was a beautiful crisp day and downtown Corpus Christi impressed. A beautiful clean city with the charm of a seaside village with a modern vibe, a very good example of where city and shoreline seem to gel together well. The numerous large birds were an incredible sight. We settled on a seafood Valentine's lunch, which seemed fitting. The boys cycled and rip-sticked for a few hours and gradually tired themselves out, a good time to go home.

Our time spent on Mustang Island was relaxing and enjoyable; when it was time to leave, we took with us some of the best memories.

About Jake's Business.

A seed was sewn the first-time breakfast was cooked for us at a campsite near The Painted Desert. Jake decided that he too could have a business serving breakfast, he thought, it could earn him some money. So encouraged, rightly or wrongly by his mum and dad, he set about planning this venture. Firstly, he wanted to be original, so no sunny side or over easy eggs for this business; he kept it simple. It was to be all about porridge. Secondly, he needed to get a handle on costs and eventually profits, therefore spending time in the supermarket noting prices of oatflakes, sugar, milk, etc. And lastly how to promote it – flyers were thought to be the most effective. When he realised Mum and Dad were not going to be the Bank of porridge, he needed to think again... Being only nine at the time, he really thought this was something that he could make happen and was disappointed to learn that certain legalities were required. However, he got on with the planning etc and who knows maybe one day he will be allowed to have his own Porridge Company!

Site 45 Chula vista
RV Resort, San Diego
CA 489760
Jan 8t 2010

The Piggy Bank,
1 Bengiman Road
Terrerbithia
USA

Dear Sir,
I would like to run a Porridge Company with your help.
My porridge Is the best porridge you will ever taste in the Whole of America,
Why now that's my secret. I am asking the bank if they could lend me $1081.
I have enclosed my business plan for you to look at.
I would like to hear from you as soon as possible.
Yours sincerely

Jake Graves

Jake's business plan bank application

THE PORRIDGE COMPANY
BUSINESS PLAN

OVERHEAD COSTS	PER DAY		
PORRIDGE	$4.00		
MILK	$2.60		
SUGAR	$1.50		
TOTAL INGREDIENTS	$8.10		
CHEF	$40.00		
SERVER	$16.00		
TOTAL WAGES	$56.00		
RENT	$10.00		
UTILILIES	$3.10		
TOTAL R & U	$13.10		
TOTAL O H PER DAY	$77.20	TOTAL OH 14 DAYS	$1,080.80
EST. PROFIT PER DAY	$112.28	EST.PROFIT 14 DAYS	$1,571.92

ESTIMATED REPAYMENT TO BANK 30 DAYS

| TOTAL LOAN REQUIRED | $1,081.00 | | |

Jakes Buisiness plan costing

Jakes business plan marketing

Pelis at Corpus Christi

GALVESTON, TEXAS

Galveston was about 280 miles from Mustang Island and we took the most direct route, but not the quickest. At the very first road sign Glen Campbell's song resonated in our minds which in turn led to singing it, eventually driving us all slightly mad. The boys deserved an explanation. Love it or hate it, the song Galveston written by Jimmy Webb is still one of the all-time Country music greats. It is a sad but beautiful love song said to be written on the beach looking over the bay, a beach that attracts many hurricanes. However, it is a war love song, some believe to be about the Spanish American war, a soldier and the girl he left behind; this explanation befits the history of the area. However, as the song was written in 1969 another account and most popular view is that of a protest song written against the Vietnam war, just a year after the Tet Offensive. Take your pick, it's still a war song and still a love song.

We drove into our campsite, the layout was a bit mixed up and confusing, but very homely. One endearing feature was the collection of four llamas in a side field just waiting for attention; they certainly had ours, such affectionate and social animals. Our coach was parked at the far side giving us a clear sea view across the road to the beach which demanded investigation. Houses on stilts similar to those of Mustang beach with chalky pastel colours giving a true seaside feel. We noticed most of the beach houses were brand new and later realised that the majority of the original houses were destroyed by the last hurricane of 2008. I'm not sure if I would be brave enough to live on the beach after that. It was a gorgeous beach with a never-ending view looking out over the Bay and the Gulf of Mexico. It is possible to walk for miles in the soft sand, which we did every morning of our stay here.

Together we investigated the background of Galveston, a conversation similar to that of Mustang Island. Named after a Spanish military leader of the 18th century, its modern history evolved after the European settlements some 200 years ago. It was a time when many immigrants landed from all over Europe, but mainly Italy and Greece. It also became home to pirates with their rich treasures, beginning the many legends which encourage children to spend hours playing and looking for these treasures. Perhaps one of the most famous narratives of them all re-counts the 1900 hurricane, known later as the Great Storm. It is still considered one of the nation's deadliest natural disasters of all time, killing up to 8000 people. It took many years to reconstruct the town as it is today and the whole place was raised by two metres. It is now a buzzing and energetic environment, although interestingly through the 1920s to '50s it was far more "risqué" as it majored in a variety of casinos and vice businesses and it earned the reputation of the Sin City of the south. Such colour, vice and intrigue. Two Italian immigrant brothers from Palermo, namely Sam and Rose Maceo, started their careers in America as barbers but found that bootlegging in the early years of Prohibition was far more lucrative. This led to them acquiring clubs which eventually developed, and the birth of the infamous Balinese Room emerged. The front entrance was built on the seawall which overlooked the water, rather grand but seemingly appropriate for the clientele it was attracting. Quite often entertainers such as Guy Lombardo, Fred Astaire, Frank Sinatra and Peggy Lee performed. The Maceos' club was also known for its outstanding cuisine. It was a high-stake casino operation which lasted until the late fifties when the courts ended all the underhand dealings and many of the operators transferred to Las Vegas, which was developing in its own right. The brothers were later well thought of by the locals as they kept out mobs, gave generously to charities, attracted regular celebrities and contributed to the overall economy.

The next day we investigated the historic downtown district with beautiful old buildings, of which surprisingly quite a few survived The Storm. A good mix of cafes, restaurants, shops and boutiques, with many museums and galleries. We found a hands-on educational area and started to investigate. The boys found a large commercial kitchen, put on their aprons and started cooking up a storm of fruit juices and breakfast, all fake of course. They moved onto more scientific games with hands-on equipment; there was a bowling alley, a writing area, and then they discovered an optician's. I think this fascinated the boys the most as one at a time they slipped into a blue doctor's coat and started to examine each other with all sorts of lookalike equipment. A few hours later we left in search of ice creams. On our way back I couldn't resist losing myself in one or two of the unusual gift shops; needless to say I purchased four martini glasses (as you do) and carefully had them packed. This now made a total of seven which needed to be transported back to Malta.

We were only in Galveston a few days but would have loved to stay longer – we were really loving this part of Texas and getting to know the barrier islands.

Old Galveston

The Opticians

DISNEY WORLD, ORLANDO

D isney was always in the plan and with Jake's 10th birthday looming up in 4 days we made our way back to Florida. The boys were all set for the long journey ahead with a home-schooling schedule to accomplish which would hopefully take away any monotony from another long road trip. Disney World, although in Mum and Dad's plan was a secret from the boys and was to be a great surprise, but first we had to get there. We planned to travel for around four to five hours on day one and we made our way towards Louisiana, driving over highway bridges including the Louisiana Bay bridge which were built over swamp lands. We eventually reached Baton Rouge. Baton Rouge is the capital of the US state of Louisiana and is found on the banks of the Mississippi in the south east of the state. Named by a French explorer Iberville back in 1699, it is said he discovered a red blood-stained pole on the bank of the Mississippi marking the borderlines between two warring native American tribes. He named the location Le Baton Rouge, which sounds charming to the English ear compared to the translation "The Red Stick".

As always with home schooling, food often found its way into discussions and we learnt that foodies today consider Baton Rouge to be a culinary destination offering two types of cuisine, creole from New Orleans and Cajun from Acadiana. Next day we moved onto De Funiak Springs, Florida, where we stayed two nights, and it was here the boys met a new friend, Austin. He too was a rip-sticker and they spent the whole day playing out, leaving their parents to organise the next few days at Disney. The next night found us at Orange Lake, Florida. The campsite itself is rated high by Woodall's (a campground directory of campsites) and we could see why. It had a golf course, heated pool, tennis courts, bike trails and more, all nestled in thoroughbred horse country. We had expected this stop to be uneventful as it was a one nighter, but alas it came with its own trauma. It was late afternoon after we parked up and organised ourselves for the night ahead. We decided to go for a long walk around the campsite, taking in the trails and the golf course. We returned to find we had locked ourselves out of our home. This was a problem. There was no way in. A small window at the front near the driver's seat was open just a fraction; however, we could not budge this. We needed help. The boy's imaginations were running riot and they were coming up with all sorts of artistic ideas, but none were practical. Keith went off to try and get help. A passer-by stopped and suggested various ways which might work, but they didn't. Then he tried to move the slightly open driver's window, gently jiggling it and pressing down. It gradually slid down and left a larger gap. He sized up the boys and his gaze fell on Josh. When he suggested that we lift Josh through the window I had all sorts of visions, one of which was his head getting stuck. Believing that what goes in must come out again is totally misguided. However, Burt, the hero of the day, convinced me Josh could do the job. I could see Jake was none too happy about this decision as he was harbouring thoughts of himself being our knight in shining armour. We got the ladder out from the under storage and Burt climbed up, I handed him Josh, and Josh somehow managed to get through the tiny gap in the window. Problem solved. Keith returned just in time to see Josh's head appear from the door as he opened it. We all thanked Burt and he went on his way. The problem we now had was Jake. He was devastated as he so wanted to be the man of the moment and for the next hour he was inconsolable and no reasoning helped, but eventually with the bribe of burgers and fries he calmed down, and all was forgotten and forgiven. Not quite the uneventful stay it was supposed to be.

With the secret still intact, we moved onto Mouse Mountain campsite, Orlando. We suggested an early night as we felt we needed our sleep. The next day was an early start and after birthday cards and birthday wishes were passed on to Jake, we suggested we all should go out for a breakfast at Pizza Hut. We knew Disney was only around six miles away, so we piled into Tobie and were on our way. The boys were very talkative in the back and missed the early signs to Disney World, but when Jake realized where we were going the anticipation raised the animation and the noise levels. We parked our old jeep in a massive car park, safe in the knowledge that it wouldn't get stolen and headed to check in and then board the boat for the short ride over to the Magic Kingdom, and as it loomed up in front of us Josh just shouted out "awesome". We could not add to that.

As we entered the Magic Kingdom we were greeted by many familiar characters; Minnie was the first with Mickey not far behind. There were balloon sellers, popcorn and candyfloss sellers, more characters, Piglet, Pooh, and all had to be negotiated before we could find our way to any sort of eating place. We found one and the boys had discovered their eating heaven. Such choices! Mac and cheese, pulled pork, foot long hot dogs, fries of all types – French fries, cheese sauce fries, chilli cheese fries, corn relish fries – that's before we found the burger choices. Jake settled for a burger and French fries, and Josh mac and cheese, Mum and Dad settled for the pulled pork, all accompanied with giant drinks, mainly sugary sodas. It was time to soak up the fun atmosphere and plan the rest of the day. As a foursome we were a mixture of opposites, Josh and Dad being of a more nervous nature preferred the slower rides designed more for the younger children, whilst Jake and myself preferred the much more aggressive grownup rides; however, we did all come together for the water rides. The first ride was a slower one which we all participated in. Inspired by the story of Alice in Wonderland and the Mad Hatter's Tea Party it involved spinning around in an enormous teacup which the spin speed you could control by a wheel inside the cup, or not. We seemed to be spinning around an even larger central teapot or cup, surrounded by trees on the outer side and many lanterns hanging from the top. It was a ride everyone enjoyed.

The next ride was also for the four of us – it was the Buzz Lightyear's Space Ranger ride. We boarded the Star Cruiser and became junior Space Rangers in the quest to stop Zurg, who was stealing batteries from helpless toys; we fired infrared laser cannons at targets. It was a ride for Josh who really loved this one.

Next up was the Railroad ride, this came with height restrictions and Jake only just made it, therefore it was a ride just for the two of us, as it was one too scary for Keith. It was a wild and very bumpy train trip racing through canyons and tunnels with falling boulders and explosions, a journey going back to the famous 1850s American gold rush times – we survived it.

Both Jake and Josh explored the Swiss Family Treehouse, climbing the wooden stairs – a total of 116 – to reach the top with views all over the Magic Kingdom, built after a shipwreck; they explored the living quarters of the family. They obviously enjoyed it as they were gone for a long time.

After drinks and snacks, it was time for the Jungle River Cruise, a ride for us all and one on which we knew we would end up rather wet. We boarded a steamer ship which took us through the Amazon of South America, it showed us the African Congo, we went along the Nile and eventually we cruised down the Mekong River in Asia, passing through waterfalls. We saw butterflies, gorillas, elephants, hippos, lions, baboons and cobras. The most frightening of all was the tribe of head hunters, but we survived heads intact.

At this stage we were beginning to flag a bit, so we decided to make our way to Liberty Square to the theatre hosting The Hall Of Presidents. A film presentation and stage show featuring Audio Animatronic figures of all the Presidents. It was great to sit down and watch a fascinating account of the story of the Constitution, the American Revolution, and the civil war. To see Abraham Lincoln on stage delivering his Gettysburg address and listening to speeches from George Washington was very impressive. Obama gave the last speech as he was the latest addition to the clan of Presidents.

Our first day at Disney World was coming to an end and we slowly made our way back towards the entrance, but we were unable to resist popping into the gift shop before we left. The boys chose some trinkets, I was eyeing up the glassware, while Keith was hovering outside impatiently looking at his watch. The boys paid for their items while I joined the end of the queue. I had noticed that throughout the Disney complex Seniors had been employed in a lot of the food and beverage outlets and also the gift shops; it was a good policy and one that seemed to be working as these Seniors were polite, helpful and lively. The old gentleman who served me apologised for being slow as this was his first day, and he needed advice occasionally from his new colleagues. He asked me if I was in a hurry. I could see Keith outside looking at his watch trying to catch my eye, but I told him no problem and to take his time – after all, everyone must learn the ropes. On learning the item – which by the way was a martini glass – was soon to be heading back to Europe, he took trouble with the bubble pack and slowly and carefully wrapped the glass and placed it in a bubble pack lined box. He wished me and my family a safe return home to Europe, I thanked him, and explained the glass would be a great addition to my collection, and that when it is used I would tell whoever the user was where it was bought and who had served me. Unfortunately to date it is my only casualty. I might have lost the glass, but I will always remember with fondness the delightful old man who served me.

We rushed to get the bus to take us to our car and to drive

the short journey back to the coach. For his birthday dinner Jake chose Chinese and we headed for the nearest Chinese restaurant. We ordered in the usual manner, which is one dish per person, plus soup plus rice. This had always worked before all over the world including Asia, but of course it was our first American Chinese, and the amount we ordered was enough for ten hungry people. It was delicious but we took good portions home with us.

It was a great day enjoyed by all and we had Day 2 in front of us.

The next day arriving at Disney World was easy, we knew the ropes. We thought we had done justice to the Magic Kingdom yesterday and so today we headed for Hollywood Studios. There was a street show of High Street Musical starting within 5 minutes of our arrival, so we found comfortable spots on the ground and waited for it to start. It didn't disappoint; the song and dance routines were familiar and superbly performed and being staged outside seemed to make it even more fun and energetic. This set the scene for the rest of the day.

The boys' names were down for some Jedi training – this is serious training by professional Jedis for 4 to 12 year olds; adults are not allowed. Outside the Jedi Temple the new recruits are given their special robes to wear whilst training, the group split into two teams for more individual training. They are trained to fight with light sabres and are well equipped to meet the dark side. Before the training is completely finished the Temple doors open with a frightening noise and slowly Darth Vader purposefully walks out and stares at the recruits. He invites them one by one to fight the dark side with light sabres and helped by their Jedi teachers they fight Darth Vader. They are exhausted when training finally ends, but lots of praise from the Jedi instructors help them recover and a certificate is received to prove their training has been completed.

With two Jedis in tow, we went to find drinks and snacks and to decide where to go next. We headed for the theatre to watch a short version of Beauty and the Beast, a vibrant and enjoyable show.

Jake and I had been eyeing up The Hollywood Hotel also known as The Twilight Zone of Terror. We decided to brave it, whilst Keith and Josh sought out a more moderate ride. We didn't really know what to expect apart from a drop of some sort, but as we approached the hotel from the side entrance we got the impression that we were in the middle of nowhere, surrounded by trees and overgrown shrubs. As we get closer to the approach, we found ourselves walking on a pavement with dry weeds growing in between the cracks. We noticed old signs pointing to the stables, a pool and further on more signs pointing the way to tennis courts, even a bowling green. It was as if we had stumbled somehow into a film set, we could faintly hear crackling music, see palm trees on each side of the road and there was a pavilion somewhat overgrown with weeds. As we approached the entrance door we looked at each other and shuddered; Jake was trying hard to look excited but admitted that it felt eerie and we had a feeling when we entered through the doors we would no longer be in control of what might happen. We became part of a story – it wasn't ours, Disney was certainly the storyteller and he told it like so.

The doors opened, the music got louder, we were met by a rather scary bellhop who ushered us into an old musty smelling foyer which we could see led into a library. We realised then that the Hotel had been closed since the 1930s and nothing had been touched or removed. It wasn't a large foyer and at the end was a marble table with Chinese style ornaments. Towards the centre there was a large carved oriental table with a lamp giving off a low light onto an Indian style silk carpet. At the side a large palm stood in a very large Chinese pot. The whole feel of the room was 1930s colonial with a bamboo ceiling fan and lights. By the front desk stood three very old suitcases, a cane walking stick was propped up by the colonial style chair and a gentleman's panama hat rested on the desk by the hotel guest book. Everything was covered in dust and cobwebs and we noticed the music was still playing; it was soft jazz style. There were notices on the run-down guest lifts suggesting they were out of order.

Two bellhops inform us guests that our rooms were not

ready and ushered us into the library area; it was very spooky. A wireless was crackling and through the open window, we noticed a storm brewing, we heard thunder and could see lightning, or perhaps it was the lights flickering. The radio crackled louder, the music faded and a voice from the radio tells a story of a stormy night in 1939. The story is about a family, a celebrity couple with their child star actress, her nanny and a hotel bellhop. The five people step into the lift and simply vanish along with the entire wing of the building. The night was remarkably similar to now and comparisons are made. The voice from the radio announces to the guests, daring them to relive that fateful night and to return with some answers, but warns that no one has lived to unveil the mystery. Tonight, the guests were told they would be the stars. We are all ushered into the service lift about to make our own story. We noticed the seats and the belts, and we were told to put on the belts and sit still. The doors suddenly closed and the lift rose to the first stop. The doors open, we can feel a cool breeze, we see just blackness at first and then faint lights. The lights are coming towards us, we are aware of the long hotel corridor. Five shapes gradually materialise and they are heading towards the service lift; they are making hand gestures for us to join them, then they disappear, the elevator door closes sharply, and once again the lift ascends and stops abruptly. The doors open again and this time there is no light, only a total blackness. A voice that seems to be very close announces: "One stormy night long ago, five people stepped through the door of an elevator and into a nightmare". The door closes abruptly again, and for the last time the lift ascends. When the doors open again, they only open halfway and we now look out towards the sky. We are so high up, we can see views stretching far past the park's entrance and further. The voice is back. "You are about to discover what lies beyond, far beyond the deepest, darkest corner of your imaginations. You are about to discover the Tower of Terror." The doors close for the last time, there is total blackness for what seems like forever, but in truth it is only a few seconds, then the elevator is plunged downwards forcing the guests off their seats, the screams surely can be heard all over Disney. The lift rises fast, and again it plunges to the depths of beyond. The guests are left in the dark for a minute, there is a scary silence, then the doors open, and we are all grateful to leave.

On leaving, Jake and I couldn't see Josh and Dad anywhere, so we decided to visit once more The Hollywood Hotel for another amazing thrill.

Josh and Dad were raving about an Extreme Stunt show that was about to start, so we made our way towards the Lights, Motors, Actions sign. A car chase through the streets of America was about to unfold. The story was about good guys being chased by bad guys; we saw stunt men falling, car chases, amazing motorbike jumps, cars set on fire, cameramen following cars – there was a large billboard TV screen showing the actual footage as it was happening. The show lasted for around 45 minutes, it was very impressive but boys' stuff.

Our time at Disney World was coming to an end but we just had time for an ice cream before heading back home. What a day.

It was Jake's birthday treat but one we will not forget.

10 today

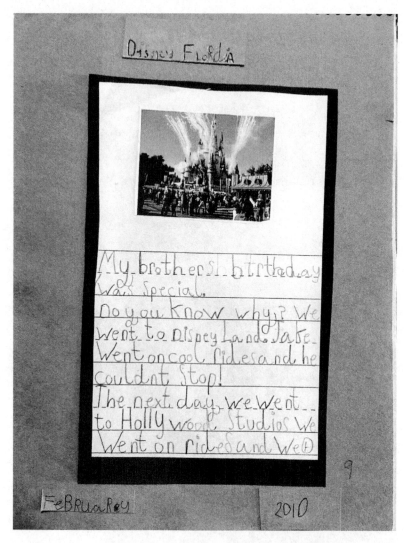

Disney Florida

My brothers birthday
was special.
Do you know why? We
went to Disney Land. Jake
went on cool rides and he
couldnt stop!
The next day we went
to Holly wood Studios we
went on rides and we

FeBRuaRey   2010

Joshies Disney diary

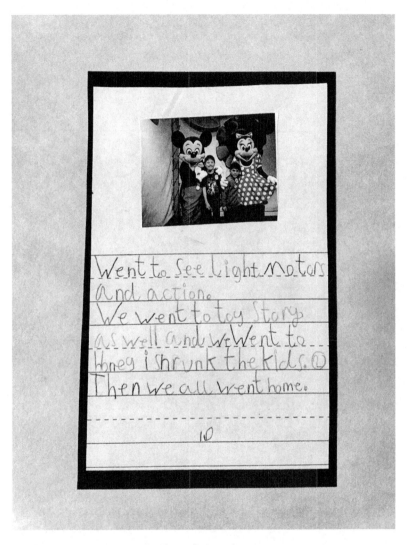

Went to see light motors and action.
We went to toy story as well and we went to honey i shrunk the kids. ☺
Then we all went home.

10

With Mickey and Minnie

This is a scary ride

Walt Minnie Goofy and Pluto

THE EVERGLADES

It was time to move towards our final destination, The Everglades, Florida. For Keith and me it was with a heavy heart as we realised that something good is nearing an end. To the boys it was just a new adventure and they were looking forward to seeing swamps and alligators. Our first stop towards this was a mere 70-odd miles from Disney World where we received a warm welcome from the very first campsite at which we stayed, Lazy Days, Tampa. Our main reason for this short visit was to investigate selling Baystar to a dealer and we went ahead and got a quote. We still had the option to sell privately should we choose. It was like returning home, everything around us seemed so familiar and we enjoyed the first-class facilities, including the pool. Our discussions with the dealers were very straightforward and we were relieved when the first price offered without too much negotiation was workable and the transaction could happen fast if we so wanted.

Our next stopover was Fort Myers where we stayed for two days to do a similar exercise. As far as home schooling was concerned, we had finished the school year and a little revision now and again was all that was required, which made it quite easy, giving us plenty of time to focus on this amazing area and its history. Fort Myers boasts of being the gateway to the South West Florida region as well as having been the winter home for Thomas Edison and Henry Ford. Thomas Edison, 1847-1931, helped build America's economy during the Industrial Revolution. From humble beginnings he rose to become a great inventor and businessman. Responsible for phonography, motion picture camera and long-lasting electric lightbulbs. Although he was not the first inventor of lightbulbs, he bought the technology to the masses. Henry Ford, 1866-1947, was famous for the Ford Motor Company, and worked for a time for Thomas Edison as an engineer before concentrating on combustion engines. He pioneered mass production and the famous assembly lines, and was also responsible for introducing better working conditions. Being British and female it's impossible for me to mention Ford without mentioning the famous strike of women machinists in 1968 at the Ford Dagenham plant in the UK, which led to the passing of the Equal Pay Act of 1970.

From Fort Myers it was another 150 miles on to Homestead, where we planned to stay for our last month. Gold Coaster Resort Homestead was a site with a difference, mainly because there were few RV places and many full-time residents in single storey mobile home-type accommodation on a very large site. Driving though the gated area it was clear we were entering a well-maintained site which was well landscaped with a pool, large clubhouse offering various games rooms, good paved roads and paths. As we drove to our reserved space, we noticed a game of horseshoes was being played and a game of Shuffleboard was in progress. These two games, we noted, were very popular in most of the RV sites we visited and of course some explanation was required as the boys were anxious to know the rules. After hooking up for a long stay, we made our way to the Horseshoe lawn and asked some appropriate questions. The game can be played either between two people or two teams of two people, known as a lawn game, but often played on a sandy beach or in a sand box area. Two stakes are set in the ground about forty feet apart and four horseshoes are used. The game is played by the players taking turns to toss the horseshoes at the stakes. Scoring is about wrapping the horseshoe around the stake. It reminded me of an old fairground game we used to play as kids.

Shuffleboard, as we later found out, is played using cue sticks which push weighted flapjacks (not the edible kind) down a narrow passage towards a marked scoring area. We were not too impressed with the game.

We decided to go walking and investigate the area away

from the camp, and it wasn't too long before we discovered what looked like a rather interesting vegetable market type of shop called Roberts. It was a great find. On entering the shop, wonderful aromas of fruit and veg pleasantly hit along with sight of vibrant colours from a huge variety of products. Apart from obvious local produce, which was in abundance, it was obvious this operation sourced much farther afield. There were many tropical fruits and veg available – it was the first time we had seen jackfruit in a long time along with Chinese lychees as well as the many other tropical fruits available. As I love to cook I could have happily amused myself for some considerable time working out recipes for these colourful fruit and veg. There was another surprise when we passed the vegetable area. I have never seen such an interesting array of jars and bottles of relishes, pickles, dressings, mustards, fruit butters, sauces, honeys, jams, jellies and spice mixes. Having decided this was worthy of my time, I started investigating and started with the honeys. Avocado honey, cinnamon honey, honey bell tangelo honey, a citrus cross between a tangerine and a pomelo, keylime and orange blossom honey, and one called Tennessee Mountain Honey – we needed an expert on this one and we were informed that it is a small tree or shrub whose leaves have a sharp acid odour due to their oxalic acid. We would probably recognise it as a sorrel tree or Lily of the valley tree. All of these honeys looked great. Next, I did the fruit butters, blueberry, apple and cherry, pecan, pumpkin, peach, strawberry, and sweet potato butters. It is no surprise that with all this unusual and interesting food there were plenty of tasters. Following the butters came the jams: apricot, blackberry, boysenberry, dutch apple, guanabana, mango jalapeno and dozens of others but the one that the boys wanted to buy was the Old Fashioned Bear Jam which we did buy, but it came after a quick English explanation of the word bear. Next came the salad dressings and there were many, blackberry and walnut, balsamic, blue cheese and walnut, apple and pecan, cranberry apple cider vinaigrette, creamy miso sesame vinaigrette, Florida orange with poppy seeds, Florida Keylime and so many more. Then came the relishes and sauces, far too numerous to remember them all, but I do remember the blackened seafood and the roasted pineapple habanero (hot chilli) sauce and the various pepper relishes, along with the chow chow relishes – which is a type of cabbage, onion and green tomato pickle. There were also many types of mustards and dips. Walking through towards the far end of the shop was the milkshake bar; the price for each shake was $5, which seemed rather excessive until we saw the enormity of a regular size drink. We did not have the stomach to contemplate a large size. The flavour selection was equally as large as it echoed all the fruits on sale. Needless to say, we each chose one; I seem to remember strawberry, keylime pie, cherry, pineapple and coconut, and vanilla were our usual choices.

We ventured outside behind the fruit market with our first huge drinks to find a seat but found much more. Best described as a mini animal farm. Wow. There were friendly goats and ostriches, ducks with their ducklings, peacocks, hens, tortoises and varieties of parrots, not forgetting the donkeys. The children were encouraged to pet and feed the goats with small bags of special food available for purchase as well as getting quite close to the ostriches. We stayed a while with the animals and the boys really didn't want to leave. I'm not too sure if I really like to see so many animals in such a small space but they did look healthy enough, so I let those thoughts go to the back of my mind. It was a most enjoyable experience and one we repeated several times in the four weeks we were at our home in Homestead Florida.

Miami was certainly on our must-visit list although a few Americans tried to warn us off as they stated it was far too dangerous to visit and certainly not a place to take young children. Having seen a few episodes of Miami Vice way back in the 80s, and as we had no intention of drug trafficking or getting involved in prostitution, we thought as a simple tourist what could be the problem – after all, Miami sees many tourists, both domestic and international, visit in a year. So, visit we planned.

We talked a little with the boys about the history of Miami, and lightened it up a bit with the mention of the movie The Birdcage. We were determined to find the building used as

The Birdcage theatre.

Interestingly enough, Miami was founded by a woman, Julia Tuttle, who was a local citrus grower, owning a lot of land. The great freeze (1894-1895) as it is known helped her develop the area as her crops were the only ones to survive in Florida. After which she then convinced the East Coast Railroad company to extend the railroad to Miami, giving her the nickname of Mother of Miami. African-Americans played a vital role in the growth of the area and by the early 20th century African-Americans, along with migrants from the Bahamas, made up 40% of the city's population. They were not allowed to reside in the city and were forced to move with threats of bombing by gangs of white men.

Miami continued to prosper during the 1920s, the population increasing and development still at the forefront. During this time many members of the police force were also members of the Ku Klux Klan (KKK), an American white hate group. Miami was certainly not a good place to live if you were black, coloured, Jewish or even Catholic – although written laws were in place more often than not they were ignored by both politicians and the police force who thought their own policies for social behaviours were superior. An example of this is when the Chief of Police publicly beat to death a coloured bellboy for directly speaking to a white woman.

Miami was also a place where many wealthy Cubans

sought refuge following the 1959 revolution, thus increasing the population further. Today Miami is an international, financial and culture centre and it has the second largest Spanish speaking population in the US.

Miami is only 35 miles away from Homestead and Bette Midler singing "Only in Miami" from her No Thrills album was played several times on the journey. It is an upbeat but sad song about a girl in Miami longing to be home in Cuba; after all, Cuba is so close but seems so far away.

If it wasn't for the film Birdcage and art deco, I'm not so sure Miami would be particularly special.

After parking our jeep amongst all the beautiful cars belonging to all the beautiful people, we were quite happy that it was perfectly safe and we made our way onto the white sandy beach with the clear blue water ahead of us. We then began exploring the Art Deco District, which in 1979 was designated as a historical district and is located in the South beach neighbourhood of Miami beach. Because of its great architectural designs, Ocean Drive has been featured on TV many times with so many of its beautiful and fun population. Italian fashion designer Gianni Versace owned a mansion on Ocean Drive. As we walked along the main street promenade, we saw many Armand and Albert types as seen in Birdcage, wearing their over-flamboyant outfits and we did find the wonderful building featured in the movie. We spent a while wandering in and out of cafes and shops, eating ice cream and soaking up the atmosphere, before heading back to the beach.

It was a good day.

The next excursion was the Everglades and it was on this morning that Josh gave a few of the early risers a giggle as they played their early morning routine game of horseshoes. The shower block was situated close to the sandy horseshoe pitch, and Josh, being a six year old boy, was never impressed with the thought of daily showering and always tried to talk himself out of the ordeal created by using soap and water. He was the only boy in the world who could have a shower without getting wet. However, this morning he decided to run ahead towards the shower block with both hands in the air shouting "you'll never catch me alive". The three elderly men probably repeated the incident at their dinner table that evening as they were still amused when we later returned from the shower block.

We set off to the Everglades themselves and it was a trip that was to be repeated many times. Together the boys had researched a lot of facts. I remember Jake being particularly interested in Ecosystems as his last project at school in Phuket was the Alpine Tundra (based on the rocky mountains, Colorado) region .We had all played a hand helping him in his creation of a diorama and we were rewarded with high marks. His explanation to Josh about ecosystems almost made Keith and I redundant in the home-schooling role. He clearly explained that the ecosystem itself is made up of both living and non-living things, forming groups of life in the area. So we have animals and plants and all other living things and rocks, sand, soil, and water, but it is how they interreact with each other that is important as it creates an ecosystem (well done that boy).

The Everglades is a vast area in southern Florida, mainly wetlands. In fact, it is actually a river very slowly making its way to the ocean, creating its own ecosystem and it covers about 1.5 million acres in all.

Interestingly and confusingly are the entrances – there are three in all, and all in separate areas of Florida and none of which we thought were connected.

Every time we visited the area, we gave the boys a financial incentive for "spotting" and as we were at the end of the dry season and the beginning of the wet, we thought this would be quite easy. Therefore, 50 "bucks" would be awarded to the first spotter of the Florida panther, 2 for spotting vultures, turtles and herons, and just 1 for alligators. Josh of course was the first to spot an alligator but sadly for the boys the Florida panther was nowhere to be seen. We saw varieties of wading birds, many of which we didn't recognise and needed some local help to identify. Each time we visited I was very uncomfortable, as the alligators seem to be quite friendly, particularly with younger and more vulnerable humans, and we had heard many tales based on the stupidity of human behaviour, involving in particular Japanese tourists who just had to have that photo of their spouse close up to the alligator – needless to say one or two didn't survive the photo shoot with a full quota of limbs. Each time we reached the visitor centre and parked the car, a ranger would warn us to look out for the vultures. Not that they were dangerous to humans: their speciality was to eat rubber. They loved eating windscreen wipers and would have a go at tyres if they could. We took care to cover up. As we were on our way out of the Everglades for the final time, Josh had his best "spot": a terrapin with rather a long tail slowly crossed the road in front of us and we were able to stop the car, get out and take photos.

We again visited the lovely old town of Fort Myers with its stunning 20th century architecture and enjoyed walking along the historic streets, ice creams in tow. We then briefly drove to Sanibel Island. We toyed with the thought that this could be our next destination but decided to keep to our original plan, which was to make our way to Malta, our final destination and our new home. Before heading back to Homestead we enjoyed time on the famous shell beach. We allowed the boys to take a shell each to add to their collection – anymore we just would not have room for.

It never ceases to amaze me how quickly it takes to accumulate so many belongings, and looking around Baystar we had many. With the thought of the imminent sale of the coach, we had to work out a plan to sell or give away our accumulated wares including the boys' bikes etc. A plan evolved for which we were granted the permission from the site management, which very much involved the boys. We organised a large yard sale of all kitchen items, including crockery, utensils, cooking pots, electric kettle etc. Plus outdoor table and chairs, books, boys' bikes and any toys they had finished with. I seem to remember all Star Wars figures were quickly hidden away from sight. It was the job of Jake and Josh to price each item, keeping all prices low for a speedy sale; they were also in charge of the selling and the negotiations with the customers. Shy at first, they soon got the hang of it and it took just two days. It was then we all realised our time touring America in our RV was coming to an end. Keith and I left the boys with their own thoughts whilst trying to sell to them our next journey, which was to be a car ride taking a few days up the East coast to New York, a distraction we thought, but it wasn't really successful. Josh was tearful and unusually quiet but was the first to come round; however, Jake took it harder and was very quiet, even short tempered, for a few days.

We drove our beloved home back to where it had all started, Lazy Days in Tampa and after some negotiation the sale of Baystar was agreed and contract signed, which gave us a few days to sell Tobie the Jeep, which we still owned. The Lazy Days executive who did the deal for Baystar made an offer for Tobie, but we felt it was far too low. We drove her to a dealer who dealt in the Jeep brand. After much negotiation a fair price was agreed and documents signed. Next day, however, we had a call from the garage saying that the guy from whom we bought the Jeep had refused to release the log book documents as he had a lien on the vehicle because we had not paid the transfer tax. Memories of dirty fingernails and shiny suited second-hand car salesmen came flooding back. The guy had conned us into thinking that he had fitted a new fuel pump before we took delivery of Tobie. This had been exposed as nonsense and we had had to pay another garage to fit a new pump when the Jeep broke down in Utah. Keith immediately got on the phone to dirty nails, pointed out the error of his ways and threatened lawyers. Lawyers put the fear of god into American second-hand car salesmen and the next day the dealership received the log book and paid us the money.

We had a few nights in the Hampton Inns and Suites where free freshly baked cookies were available all day long, something to bring a smile to Jake's face.

Geoffery

Roberts

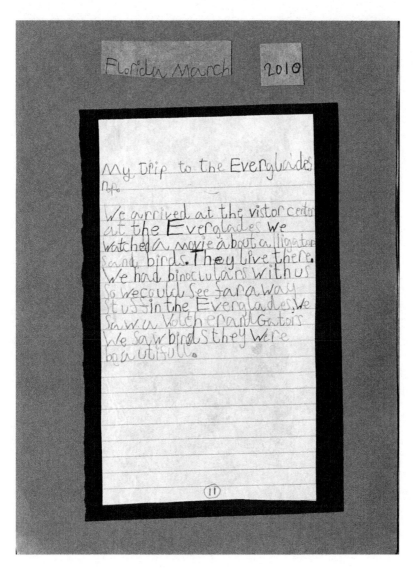

Florida March 2010

My trip to the Everglades
nps

We arrived at the vistor center
at the Everglades we
watched a movie about alligator
sand birds. They live there.
We had binoculars with us
so we could see far away
st uss in the Everglades. We
saw a volth er and Gators
we saw birds they were
beautifull.

(11)

Joshes Everglades diary

Joshie Everglades wildlife

TOWARDS MANHATTAN

The day before we left for our journey up the East coast towards New York, a huge shiny burgundy coloured Buick rental car was delivered to us in preparation for the next few days' road trip. It looked a comfortable car and one that would take us all the way to New York with all our kit, but I'm not too sure Jake was impressed with the model – however, an estate car is what it is, useful. We had rather a lot of luggage, therefore were in desperate need of good trunk/boot space. It certainly looked the part. We reckoned it was approximately 1,100 miles to the hotel we had booked in New York, which was a Holiday Inn close to Newark airport. We thought it sensible to stay close to the airport as problems were occurring with all flights due to an ash cloud from an erupting volcano in Iceland; in addition, transport into Manhattan from Newark was easy. We planned to split the journey, stopping a night in Savannah, Georgia and two nights in Washington DC, a must before our final stop, New York.

We left immediately after an early breakfast as it was to be a fairly long drive, approximately 330 miles to Savannah, which we estimated would take around 5-6 hours plus a stop. The drive would take us across Florida from the west to the east side, close to Jacksonville, which is around 25miles south of the Georgia State Line. Ask any parent and they will tell you that a long car journey isn't always easy with energetic children, and this one had the makings of an horrendous affair. The tell-tale signs were there. The ownership of backseat space was an issue, so an invisible line was drawn, then there was the argument about who took the most cookies from the hotel lobby for the journey, therefore the eating of cookies were banned until the first stop. Then, who had the most important of the Star Wars figures. There was no solution to that one and the constant bickering between two naturally competitive children who are thrown together early in the morning in a confined space continued. So, after a while a few miles of my bad navigating, and Keith finding his way around the sat-nav, a story was required. This time the request was for A message in a bottle, one I had told many times with various endings. I was getting quite bored with this one, but the boys added some new twists – the story must include secrets, and the White House. At least that gave me something to work on, the stars of the story remained the same, of course, and we settled down once again to a 'Once Upon A Time' story which I made last all the way to New York.

A Message in a Bottle.

Once Upon A Time...There were two best friends, Jake, and Josh, they had been friends forever, they couldn't even remember a time they hadn't known each other. The truth is they met at nursery school at the age of 3 and had been buddies ever since. It helped that they lived in the same Avenue, a rather stylish one with the name Beaux Arbres, a name often heard linked with words like desirable and sought after. In truth the location was of little interest to the boys, who at eight years old would live anywhere if only they could be next door neighbours; however, they had to make do with a ten minute bike ride which was how long it took to get from one end of the Avenue to the other, Jake's house being the first in the street and Josh's the last. The boys were also members of the same kids' gym club, and often shared the same interests, the latest being Manga. They both went to the same school and both had the burden of a younger sister aged five. Because of their friendship, their mums had become good friends too, which of course helped in many ways, particularly when it came to sleepovers. They lived in Washington DC and were only a ten-minute drive or a 30-minute walk to the

White House, which meant that politics hung in the air, it was often said, like pollution.

Reporting directly to the President of the United States, Josh's father held the position of Secretary of Education, a position he had held for eighteen months. As Josh had admitted to his friend, he wasn't particularly impressed with his father's job and secretly thought that his father was pretty useless at it – after all, who had ever heard of a secretary who didn't even type? But Josh was learning more and was slowly changing his opinion. Jake was continually fascinated when his friend told stories about the goings on in the White House, he was always sworn to secrecy and never breathed a word to anyone. In truth his friend Josh listened at doors when his parents were having the most private conversations and combined with his youth and imagination, he told the most amazing stories. Josh, on the other hand, was far more impressed with Jake's father who was a successful heart surgeon, and quite famous too. He was recently asked by the Japanese government to oversee a training programme advising Japan's top heart surgeons of the new techniques being used in America. Jake just hoped the family would not have to relocate to Japan, as he loved his life in Washington DC and wanted to stay put for the rest of his life.

Tonight, they were sleeping over at Josh's house; they always looked forward to these nights as they would stay up late, sneak food from the pantry and have midnight feasts. But tonight, unusually, they were under strict instructions from both sets of parents to have an early night as they needed to be fresh for the next day. Tomorrow was Friday and the day of the school outing. Both boys were excited. It was traditional in their school that the Grade 3s have a yearly White House visit. At last it was their turn. Jake was more excited than Josh as he secretly harboured a dream of working in the White House one day, but he kept that to himself. Try as they might, sleep alluded them, so they drifted into quiet conversation. This evening it was Jake's turn to let one of his secrets slip. It was a secret he hoped he would never regret sharing with his friend, but of course he could trust Josh with his life. There was a girl in grade 4 whom he very secretly liked. Her name was Tania. He had never spoken with her as he was terrified of being laughed at, also she was much older than him. This shocked Josh to the core; he never envisaged his best friend even thinking about girls let alone this one whom he knew to be totally off limits. Of all the girls he could choose, why oh why did he have to like Tania? "You know she is totally out of bounds," Josh sternly told Jake, who nodded and wondered if that was the reason he liked her so much. The two boys eventually fell asleep, having talked through the WHT problem which was to be their code name for Tania.

Organising a trip to the White House involved a lot of paperwork and preparation by the school – for example, any request to visit must come through a member of congress who agrees to issue the tickets. Group photos and individual photos must be taken before the visit, along with many forms to be completed by the parents in triplicate. All this organising happened six months in advance. Josh explained that the Secret Service needed time to check out each of the coming visitors and to refuse anyone who is likely to be a threat to the President of The United States. Josh also broke the annoying news that the President was away on a state trip, so there was no chance of meeting him. This was a blow to Jake who was so looking forward to shaking his hand.

The next day they met up with their class teachers and friends before boarding the coach that was to take them a short 15-minute ride to the White House. The instructions were very clear. All bags and packed lunches etc were to be left in the coach, all pockets were to be empty except for a handkerchief ,and if necessary, glasses in a glasses case. They were also told that once inside the White House there were no public bathrooms, therefore there would be a trip to restrooms before the security checks. With excitement in the air, the children boarded the coach and were driven to 15 Street NW where the coach was to be parked.

On arrival the children were in awe of the Secret Service and a little frightened when they were all requested to show their ID and have it checked against each child. Next, they had to line up and wait for what seemed forever to have their individual photos taken, then more lining up in preparation to go through a metal detector like those at an airport. At last they were given the all-clear and were ready to go and explore. The secret service men smiled and gestured for the teachers and children to go forward into the corridor towards the East Wing.

The corridor was long and the walls full of pictures and photographs. The teachers asked the children to look carefully at them to see if they could identify any of the past presidents, or past presidents' families; they also noted that there were even some photos of past presidents' pets. It was fascinating, particularly to Josh as he had grown up with talk about past presidents, their accomplishments and even their scandals and he was surprised when he realised just how much he knew. He thought he may have many questions for his dad next Sunday lunchtime which was a time when no subject seemed off limits. As for Jake, he was just stunned at the opulence and the feeling of luxury and richness which seemed to penetrate through the whole White House. WOW, he thought. Awesome.

They walked on to the Library Room and noted that whilst visitors were not allowed inside any of the rooms, they could peek inside to their hearts' content. One teacher explained that this was a room often used for informal meetings and afternoon tea by both the President and the First Lady. Jake was just envisioning Tania drinking tea with her parents when the teacher went on to point out a lighthouse clock that had been made by John Willard, who was a famous clockmaker of years gone by. Personally, both boys thought the clock ugly, and spoilt a rather cosy room which included a fireplace and wood panelling.

The next room was named the China Room, but when the boys realised it was about cups, saucers, and plates they rather lost interest. This room housed the entire White House collection of State china and was rather grand as the origins of the crockery included China, France, and America to name a few. They wondered on to the East Room. This room, they were told, was the largest in the White House, a room where history is made. It has been used for a variety of events and ceremonies over the years, including hosting music events, wedding ceremonies, even funerals, and often the room where important announcements are made.

The green room was next, another reception room where cocktails are served. The boys hoped they were not going to be tested on all these rooms as one was beginning to merge into the next. Then came the blue room and they had to admit this was the most elegant room of all, with wonderful views looking over the south lawn. This room was full of antiques and decorated in French Empire style. This is the famous room where the White House Christmas tree is located. Josh had shown Jake each year photos of the tree and hoped one year they would be invited to help decorate it, but that was in the future.

The last room they visited was the Red room which was small and quite cosy and often used by the first ladies when entertaining friends and guests. Decorated in American Empire style, it had accents of Greek and Egyptian style furniture. It was in this room that Jake noticed a painting of a family sitting around a table about to eat food. The painting was simply named 'Everyday Feast' and the artist was Alberto Vildo. The food looked amazing and so very real; it was almost as if the artist was inviting you to take food from the massive highly decorated serving dish that lay in the centre of the table. The table itself was quite plain in contrast and carved out of a dark wood that had been highly polished. There seated were two adults, presumably Mum and Dad, and their children, a boy and girl. In front of each of them lay a lace table mat and a rather heavy and ugly looking knife and fork. By the side of the serving dish was a cruet set, or he thought that was what it was called as his grandmother had one just like it. This consisted of an open salt cellar, a pepper pot, and a glass dish that Jake thought could be used for mustard. It was funny, he thought, that there was an empty space where he imagined a vinegar bottle should be. He noticed the look on the family's faces and wondered why the artist had made the Mum and Dad look shocked and the children quite frightened and very unhappy, but he thought perhaps this Alberto Vildo just didn't know how to paint faces properly. His friend came by his side and suggested they both move on. Jake pointed the painting out to Josh who was not particularly impressed but did agree about the food, it really did look quite real. A large selection of meats in a reddish sauce with purple and green vegetables they thought to be aubergines and spinach plus some rice, and at the far side of the plate lay rather a rustic looking loaf. Josh noticed that some of the sauce had spilled onto one of the lace table mats, funny they thought and wondered why the stained mat had been painted in the first place. Jake concluded that this painting was probably there to hide a blemish on the wall and the White House had run out of decent paintings.

They were moved on by two secret service agents who suggested they catch up with their teachers, but Josh plucked up the courage and asked if they would be allowed to get a glimpse of the Oval Office. Jake let out a gasp at the boldness of his friend, but the secret service agents just smiled at the boys and suggested they come back another time having pre booked a tour around the Oval Office. Satisfied with that, they joined their classmates in the White House garden and walked towards what was known as the First Lady's vegetable garden. Here the children were encouraged to plant some vegetables; there were a few choices, but most chose to plant potatoes. They got on with the job and started digging. They were supervised by the White House gardeners and certainly encouraged with much enthusiasm. Each child left determined to plant vegetables in their own gardens, maybe this weekend. As they were returning their tools to the shed ready for the next lot of children, Josh stumbled on a rather large stone and heard a cracking sound; he immediately looked down and saw a muddy container with what looked like a rather dirty looking grasshopper inside. Josh loved any sort of bugs and the thought of owning a special White House bug just took over his thought process and he immediately picked up the container and placed it in his trouser pocket.

By the time they left the White House it was lunchtime and the children headed back to their coach, picked up their lunches and walked in the direction of Capitol Hill, where they found a space on the lawn to have their picnic. The teachers gave them each a folder to take home and work on over the weekend; it consisted of a few easy questions and they were asked to give an account of the day or to write a short story involving the White House. On reflection both boys thought they had got off quite lightly, particularly as it was a long weekend. When they returned to school Jake's mum was waiting for both boys as it was agreed that Josh would stay over for both Friday and Saturday nights, returning home first thing on Sunday morning in time for church. They stopped by Josh's house to pick up his bike and overnight stuff; they were now set for the weekend. It was suggested by Jake's mum they get their homework completed and out of the way. They both nodded in agreement but of course this never happened.

They were settled in Jake's bedroom with a drink and some snacks when Josh remembered the bug he had deposited in his pocket. He told his friend who was astonished he had managed to smuggle out a White House bug under the close scrutiny of the Secret Service; both boys went into fits of giggles and wondered if Josh had been recorded on camera doing the unlawful deed. When Josh picked up his jacket, he was a bit concerned as the pocket was moving and he said he thought it was a brown grasshopper but he never really took a good look at it. Josh tipped the container on the floor gently and they both took a closer look. The container was covered in mud and was cylindrical and it rolled on the soft carpet. "Hey You! Stop that, I'm getting dizzy. What do you think you're doing?" Astonished Jake was the first to comment as he looked at his friend, and they both took a step back. "It spoke, the bug spoke," he whispered. Now this so-called bug was quite indignant. "Who are you calling a bug, how rude you are. First of all you take me from my home, put me in a smelly dark place and then roll me around quite roughly. Who are you anyway?" Now it was Josh's turn to be indignant. "My pockets are not smelly, and the one you were in was empty except for my gum which I hope you didn't chew on." The bug was just about to retort when Jake gently asked his name. "You can address me as Donio 1st," he said proudly. The boys just looked at each other, but Josh just had to ask, "Does that mean there is a second, third and maybe a fourth?" Donio 1st rather superiorly replied that there were in fact 24 of them and being the first almost amounted to royalty. He shifted rather uncomfortably as he was confined to such a small space and could not move much. The boys then made their introductions to Donio 1st. It was Josh who suggested to him that he should come out of the container or whatever it was, and show himself. He was wanting to see what this Donio 1st looked like. This time Donio 1st tried to look in Jake's direction as he said, "Is he for real, or maybe he thinks so-called 'bugs' like me have some sort of glass fetish that we need to be stuck for ever in a bottle." It was then that it dawned on the boys that this so-called container was actually a glass bottle and the truth of the matter was that Donio 1st was indeed truly stuck inside. Josh wanted to make amends and assist this creature in whatever way he could. He asked simply, "How can we help get you out?" Donio 1st sighed, and said that he really didn't know, he had been trying for what seemed like forever, and it always came back to the same problem. It was his head; it was just too big. "I know, I know, you both are wondering how I got into this mess in the first place, but the truth of the matter is, what goes in doesn't necessarily come out again." "Oh" was the reaction of both boys. Jake was not so sure if this were true, but it certainly was a problem and this problem, he thought, might end up being theirs.

First things first, this container/bottle needed to be cleaned up as it was caked in White House garden mud and they needed to see the problem as it is. So, gently, Jake lifted the bottle and took it to the bathroom where he proceeded to gently wipe down the outside, explaining each move to Donio 1st as it happened. It took a while but eventually the bottle was sparkling clean. It was a shock for both the boys and for Donio 1st who didn't realise the boys were quite as small as they were, and the boys thought that Donio 1st despite his protestations was still some kind of bug, maybe a modern bug? But bug he was not.

Jake stood the bottle up so Donio 1st could stand on his feet. It was Josh who recovered first. "Please forgive us for thinking you were a bug, we had no idea that you could possibly be, well, a, mini, um, well I guess a smaller version of us, just a bit older."

Jake added that although they had heard of leprechauns, which they believed to live in Ireland, they didn't realise leprechauns had an all American version here in Washington DC. It was now Donio 1st's time to speak. He smiled at the boys. "Well the top of the morning to you now." He was pleased to see the boys giggling, but reverted back to his own voice, which was a mixture of American and Italian with a hint of a soft lilt that could almost be Irish. "Why, I am so relieved to find you are young boys as they are always so much fun and a little bit naughty, but I have to be honest, you are the first of the 'Watchits' I have had the pleasure to meet and actually talk to, as we are forbidden to make ourselves known to any "Watchit". But you see it wasn't me who made myself known to you, now did I? It was you who took me from my home." As he said this he was looking at Josh who reddened, but he went on to say, still looking at Josh, "I guess you could make amends by getting me out of this bottle, and if you do that we can call it quits."

"If we do that, we will become your heroes," Jake quickly and firmly responded to defend his friend. Actually, Jake went on to make a deal with Donio 1st. They agreed that when Donio 1st was free of the bottle he would share with them his story, which they all admitted would be quite something, and they did so want an explanation for "Watchits". Also, Josh asked if he could drop the 1st as Donio was more friendly, and it was agreed.

But back to the business in hand, how to free Donio from his prison? The boys gave it much thought and wondered if Vaseline could be the answer. They rubbed a little on the inside neck of the bottle and suggested that Donio rub a little on his ears and sides of his head. He was not happy about this, but Jake promised him he could have a wash later to remove all the grease. Donio raised his arms to the top of the bottle while Josh, using his finger and thumb, tried to pull Donio gently out of the bottle. He failed; Jake took over and tried many times to ease Donio out, but he too failed. Josh tried again, Jake tried again; it was useless. Josh then had the idea to somehow break the bottle. "No, No, No," cried Donio. Josh tried to assure him that he could break the glass without hurting him at all.

"You just don't understand, it's not my bottle and I need to return it, it must go back."

The boys didn't mention or ask how Donio would get the bottle back to the White House, assuming this was where it was from, as the bottle was as big as him, but they had the feeling this was another problem they would have to help solve.

Josh had an idea and asked Jake if he still had his old glass cutting set, he had been given one year for a Christmas present.

"Glass cutting, did you say glass cutting? I've already told you, you cannot cut the glass. Aren't you two listening to a word I'm saying? I can see I'm wasting my breath and time." Donio's tone was more scared than cross but Jake was cross.

"Now you listen here, you little man or whatever you are, we are trying hard to help you." He looked over at Josh as he said, "Yes, I think I still have the kit, but you were so much better at it than me, it's worth a try."

Before Donio could comment, Josh suggested they all have a look at the kit and decide if it's possible. He then went on to explain to Donio that if they can make a clean cut it was quite easy to repair without the join being too obvious. Both boys hunted for the set which they found at the bottom of the wardrobe, right at the back. Josh opened the box and got out the relevant tools, a board, a knife resembling a scalpel, magnifying glass, rulers, eyeglasses, glue. Looking at Jake he asked, "What do you think?" What Jake really thought he kept to himself, but looking in the direction of Donio he smiled and tried to convince him that it could work. Josh readily agreed as he did really think he could make it work.

Donio wasn't convinced. "It's all right for you two, but supposing when cutting the glass your hand slips, you could cut me clean in half, then where would I be, in two pieces; you would probably feed me to the birds."

"Don't be silly," Josh retorted, losing patience. He gently picked up the bottle to have a good look, picked up the magnifying glass and peered into the bottle looking for possible places to cut that would be easy to repair. This made Donio nearly jump out of his skin then he felt a little queasy as Josh's eyeball increased in size and he could see the bright blueness of his eyes; he had to shield his face.

"Donio," Josh explained, "if you were to crouch down and get as small as you can, you would be quite safe. Take a look at this diamond pattern at the back of the bottle. If I were to completely cut this out do you think it would be a big enough space for you to climb out of?"

Donio scrutinised the diamond shape and measured his head against the glass. "Yes, I could get through that, easy, but are you sure you can put the piece of glass back again?"

Both boys assured him that this was no problem, a piece of cake even. Donio wasn't sure what cake had to do with it, but he was reminded just how hungry he was, having survived on raw potatoes and zucchini leaves for so long. He was going to mention this to the boys but thought better of it as he didn't want to get fat until he was safely out of the bottle.

It was then that the sound of footsteps could be heard coming up the stairs. Jake quickly grabbed Donio and hid him and his bottle under the bed, giving him strict instructions not to mutter a word. The door opened, and Jake's mum came into the room, pleased to see the boys playing with something other than computer games. She smiled and told them to come down for dinner in 30 minutes. The boys agreed and listened as they heard her footsteps returning downstairs. They quickly got to work; they prepared the desk for the 'operation'. Josh donned the glasses, and picked up the bottle with a terrified Donio crouching at the bottom in the smallest ball he could muster. Jake tried to offer some sort of comfort to Donio, telling him all was going to be just fine. Josh gently scored around the diamond shape, realising the glass itself was a bit tough he had to do this a few times, but it was beginning to come loose and he very slowly put his finger into the bottle and eased out the diamond shape. Donio stood up, realised he was in one piece and smiled at the boys. "You did it then."

The boys were pleased with themselves, but there was another problem to solve: how to get Donio out of the bottle without him cutting him to shreds. They wrapped toilet paper around the opening, Jake took hold of Donio's arms with his fingers and gently lifted him out through the diamond hole onto the carpet. "Wow," was all Donio could say and he proceeded to run, jump, and do somersaults on the carpet until he fell over. The boys could not stop laughing at this endearing little man until there were tears in their eyes. Donio then shyly asked if he could wash or bathe as he was covered in the White House mud, also he could feel the Vaseline all over his hair and ears. Jake made a bubble bath for him using the soap dish, he placed it on the floor in the bathroom, and gave him the smallest towel he could find, which was a face towel. Josh suggested they should wash his clothes later as he thought they would be dry in no time. They looked at their watch, it was dinner time, so they left Donio to luxuriate in his bath while they went down to dinner.

It was BBQ night which was always a favourite and the boys settled down to their burgers and salad. Jake's mum and dad were making jokes with the boys and asking about their day at the White House. But where was Natasha? The boys did not really care but it seemed to worry Jake's mum, who left the garden and called out her daughter's name. Jake knew he loved his sister Natasha, but he wasn't too sure if he actually liked her – she was always spying on him, and told many stories that he just knew weren't true; he always had to look out for her which she didn't really deserve, but hey, he had learnt to live with it. She eventually arrived with her mum in tow and joined them at the table. All was OK until it was time for the trifle to be served when Natasha blurted out that she had a secret.

"We all have some secrets, Natasha, but just remember, if you tell a secret it's no longer a secret anymore," her father sensibly said.

Natasha kept on going and said that this secret shouldn't be a secret anyway, as it wasn't her secret, therefore, she would tell it. Then came the bolt from the sky. "There is a naked man in the soap dish having a bath in Jake's bathroom on the floor," she announced quite dramatically as only a five-year-old girl can.

Jake's mum and dad laughed out loud while the boys nearly spat out their trifle. It was Josh who normalised the situation by telling the story his sister Amy had told just yesterday when she tried to convince everyone that she had a tree in her bedroom that only grew at night time and this tree produces the most amazing liquorice. This of course made everyone laugh except for Natasha herself, who insisted her story was true and that she could quite easily get proof. Jake's mum had to gently remind Natasha of the chat they recently had about going into Jake's room without his permission, so the subject was changed and the boys, although on high alert, enjoyed their second portion of trifle.

They returned to Jake's room to find an angry and quite frightened Donio. They found him crouched behind the washbasin, gripping his enormous towel; he looked most vulnerable.

"So, you've met my sister Natasha then, she's really quite harmless but just a bit of a pain." Jake's tone was so apologetic even Donio must realise how difficult it is to live with a sister like Natasha.

Donio explained, he was so enjoying his bath, washing his hair, smelling of what he only could describe as a meadow of flowers when this baby girl, barged in the bathroom, looked at him in all his naked glory, squealed with laughter, pointed at him and ran out. "Thank goodness your mother didn't find me."

The boys were relieved too, but Josh wondered why Natasha should go into the bathroom in the first place. "Ah, that might be my fault, it's a typical Donio trait, you see we all sing in the bath, all, being my entire family, even the girls." It was agreed, that perhaps it was a bit foolish, but now they needed to move on and fast.

A 'Natasha-proof' hiding place must be found, a bed must be organised for Donio, clothes must be washed, and the most important of all, the glass bottle must be fixed. Jake found an old cloth hanky which he cut, handed it to Donio 1st, and told him to make a sarong type of garment, while Josh proceeded to glue together the diamond piece of glass back where it came from. Meanwhile Jake was busy washing Donio's clothes and he was surprised to find that they weren't brown in colour after all, but the jacket was a bright burnt orange, the trousers were a deep red, and his socks were a greyish white. He cleaned the tiny shoes, and tried to shine them on the towel, then, using his hairdryer he carefully dried Donio's tiny outfit. He then went about the task of making a bed up for Donio. He used a small boiled sweet tin that was full of chewed up gum, cleaned it, lined it with toilet paper, cut the remainder of the hanky in two and used the pieces as a top and bottom sheet. All done, he looked over at Josh and found that the bottle was back together on top of his bookshelf drying nicely. Josh lifted Donio to show him the bottle. He scrutinised every angle but just could not see the join. He looked over at the boys with tears in his eyes. "I don't know what to say, but thank you both so much, you have no idea what this means, not just to me. You are both truly my heroes, and now deserve to be told my story, if it's not too late in the evening as it is a long story."

The boys looked at their watches, it was only 8.00, plenty of time, but before that they needed to get food and drink for Donio and snacks for themselves. Jake went downstairs whilst Josh stood guard in the room. When he returned, the room was secured by placing a pile of books by the door.

They settled down with their food and drink, looking forward to the story of Donio 1st. The boys thought he looked simply splendid in his clean clothes. First, Donio needed promises from the boys never to repeat a word of his story, because it is not just his story, it's a White House story as well with so many real secrets. The boys solemnly promised and crossed their hearts and hoped to die, which secretly Donio thought was going too far but didn't say anything. "Oh dear, where to start..." but Josh thought it best to start at the very beginning, and they promised not to interrupt. "That is good, because some of the things I must tell, you may not believe at first," Donio warned.

"We call ourselves Lookits, we don't know where we came from but there is a theory. The original White House architect was a man called James Holborn, who was born in Ireland and was asked to design a house fit for a president. He did, this took a long time, but he finally got the agreement to go ahead. Being Irish, he was lonely, he longed for Ireland and the little people. One night he had a dream that the Irish leprechauns sent to him his own American Little People. The next day he awoke to the sight of eight little people sitting on his bed, they told him they were called Lookits, meaning lookouts, meaning they were going to protect him. Now whether this is true or not, you have got to agree it is rather a romantic story, and we Lookits like to believe it's true." Both the boys nodded in agreement.

"Now, as you both know the White House has seen many Presidents, some good some not so good, but in their way have all left a mark on America and the White House. You must have heard the rumours about ghosts of old presidents being seen – well, I can tell you, that is because some of our

"Lookits" were not doing their jobs properly on the night the ghosts were seen. Because it is our job to protect both the ghosts and the residents of the White House, it is our job to keep them apart from each other. There are certain Presidents who are constantly teasing us; they certainly keep us on our toes. It would take me forever to go through all the ghosts of the old Presidents, but the ones that have been seen the most are The Ghost of Abraham Lincoln as well as the ghost of the wife of John Adams. Her name is Abigail. This is the oldest ghost to be seen, as her husband was only the second president. She used what is now the East room as her laundry room because it was the warmest in the house. She has been reported walking, dressed in a long grey dress, white apron, cap and lace shawl, her arms are always outstretched as if carrying a large laundry basket."

Josh could not help himself as he interrupted, "Oh Donio please tell us about Abraham Lincoln's ghost."

Donio 1st just laughed. "OK, there have been a few sightings, perhaps the most famous is when his ghost appeared to the British Prime minister Winston Churchill – you don't really need me to tell this tale as you can look it up for yourselves in any history book as they all tell the same story almost word for word. He, that is Winston, had finished a lengthy dinner with the President who was Roosevelt, Franklin that is. They left each other in the early hours of the morning and said goodnight. Winston, as he always did each night, luxuriated in a long hot bath, sipping a large brandy and smoking his cigar. He got out of the bath, placing his brandy and cigar down, dried and powdered himself, combed his hair, retrieved both brandy and cigar, and walked naked into his adjoining bedroom. He was startled to see Lincoln standing at the fireplace leaning on the mantle looking towards Winston. In true Churchill style he quickly recovered, took the cigar out of his mouth, and said, "Good evening, Mr President, you seem to have me at a disadvantage." President Lincoln just smiled, then laughed before disappearing."

Both Jake and Josh found this story very funny; they were not too sure who this Winston Churchill was, but they certainly liked his style. They all stopped for a while so they could drink and snack.

"By the way we call all residents, employees, and visitors to the Whitehouse Watchits, because we watch out for them, and all the ghosts we simply call hauntits. That is the way it has always been. We have always lived at the White House and the White House has always looked after us. That is, all 169 of us. Food is plentiful, although it always involves a lot of climbing and our living quarters are most comfortable."

Jake was just going to asked how on earth he ended up in a glass bottle, when the story continued.

"About six months ago, I'm not sure whether you know this, but a burglary took place at the White House, it was very much hushed up at the time for security reasons. The burglars had intended to steal many of the paintings, most of which are originals, but fortunately they only got away with a few. They cut the main power and both the generators, also the emergency power. The Lookits were the first on the scene and called upon the Hauntits to help. The idea was amazingly simple: the Hauntits were to frighten the Watchits with their noises and weird appearances. Well, unbeknown to the Lookits, the Hauntits were able to change their appearances and they became the most frightening creatures imaginable, they could even fly, and charged into the burglars who were terrified and literally ran for their lives, leaving most of the paintings behind. Now, and here is what happened to me. I was standing just inside the red room, when one of the burglars went to grab a painting – it was the painting I happened to be standing under. The burglar saw a flying raptor lookalike and was frightened out of his life. We think it was President Nixon's hauntit but we can't be sure. The painting over my head dropped to the floor. It was a painting of a family sitting around a table at dinner time."

Jake took an intake of breath. "Oh my, the vinegar bottle is missing from the table."

Donio was really impressed. "You must be the only person who has noticed it missing."

It was Josh's turn to speak. "There was food spilt on the table mat. That must have been because the painting fell."

Donio smiled as he realized the boys were very switched

on. "Why yes, it did fall, I moved out of the way, but the bottle fell right on top of me and I ended up inside. The food rolled off the table but one of the children grabbed it and put it back the best she could, meanwhile the mum and dad were clinging onto both table and each other. When the painting landed on the floor, they tried to help me but could not. They pleaded with me to get help to get out of the bottle, and return the bottle to the painting, because without the bottle the painting wouldn't be complete. If a painting is not complete it reverts back to just paint and brush strokes. This means the family does not exist. If a painting is incomplete for over a year it is too late. So, do you see now why I must return the bottle to the painting so that the family can live again?"

Wow, this was some story. They needed to think about this seriously – how on earth were they going to return Donio to the White House with the bottle? It was getting extremely late, and they needed their sleep. They decided to forget the problem for now and rethink the situation in the morning.

They slept late, but after breakfast they decided to go for a walk away from the house and any nosy 5-year-old sister. Josh carefully put Donio in the side pocket of his rucksack and off they went to their local park where they found a very private spot and sat down to talk.

Jake was the first one to speak. "Couldn't we get both the bottle and Donio to the White House via your dad's brief case, or pocket?" As soon as he said it he realised that this wouldn't work because the problem was really how to put the bottle back in the painting, Donio was too small and he couldn't envisage Josh's dad going along with any of this.

Then Josh had the brainwave of WHT. Donio was confused. "It's our code word for Tania, i.e. White, House, Tania. We would have to let Tania in on our secret." But could they really trust a girl?

This time Donio had something to say. "No, No, and No, not Tania. Don't forget I know the family well, I have often had to look out for the family, and Tania is not the answer, absolutely NO."

Jake wondered why Donio didn't like or trust Tania.

"It's nothing to do with liking or trusting, she is just too old; her first reaction would be to tell her father, they are very close you know."

Jake didn't agree that she was too old as she was only 18 months older than him, but Donio explained, "she's a girl and in girl years at her age she is 4 years older than you boys and cannot be trusted at all".

They all went silent for a while, but it was Donio's turn to have an idea. "What about her younger sister Anna? She is not too old, in fact I'm sure she will help us, she is at that age when everything is an adventure and I know she can keep secrets."

The boys were uneasy about this as she was incredibly young – could she really be trusted? Donio was certain she could, and the boys would just have to take his word for it. OK, if it were going to be Anna, how on earth could they contact her as all calls were screened by the Secret Service, and bodyguards went everywhere with her, even at school. Donio thought she went to the gym every evening for swimming. "How about we all hang around the gym and try and get her attention?" The boys had their reservations but kept them to themselves. A plan was eventually hatched. Early in the evening they headed off to the gym for a "chance" meeting with Anna. They were in luck as she was there with her friend who left first. Jake approached her quietly and asked if he and his friend could ask a big favour. His heart was pounding as he was expecting to get arrested any minute by her bodyguards, but they didn't seem to take too much notice. She smiled at him as she recognised him from school, he handed her a bag of candy and they started to talk. Josh came over and joined in, but Donio was hidden out of sight for the time being. They told the whole story and were surprised she didn't accuse them of making it all up, she didn't even seem to be shocked.

She smiled at them as she said, "I suppose you want me to put the bottle back in the painting, I know which painting you mean; it's the one of the miserable family, and the food. Now I know why they are so miserable! Of course I'll help, on one condition."

The boys just looked at each other and nodded.

"You reveal Donio 1st to me now."

Nobody said anything for a while until Donio 1st appeared

from the top of Jake's pocket. He climbed out with a little help. She just stared at him for a while and with her amazing smile she said, "Donio 1st, I must thank you for looking out for all of us at the White House and in return I will return you to your home and return the bottle to the painting."

The boys and Donio were relieved.

"It's best if I take you with me now as Dad, that is The President, is away, Tania is at a party and there's only Mum, The First Lady, at home, so I would be able to sneak into the other side of the house. Donio 1st, you will be able to show me the secret passages that lead to the Red Room, so I do not get caught."

It was happening too fast for the boys who were rather taken with Anna's complete common sense and decisiveness. Donio was right about Anna.

Jake, Josh and Donio had only known each other for just over 24 hours, but it seemed like they had been friends for so much longer. They realised they needed to say their goodbyes. This was it. They hugged, promised to keep all secrets safe and sadly said goodbye for the last time. Anna promised she would have both Donio 1st and the bottle back in place by tonight. She would leave a message at the gym for them tomorrow to pick up. They noticed 2 of her bodyguards approach, so they roughly handed Donio 1st to Anna, who quickly put him in her gym shoe. No one heard the protestations of Donio 1st.

Josh returned to his home on Sunday morning, but the

boys met at the gym that evening and enquired if there was a message for them. There was a rather large envelope, addressed to both boys, and inside was a small empty perfume bottle with a piece of paper inside. The note just said: 'All is well, the little Lookit is back to work, he is now a hero. A family we know are enjoying vinegar with smiles to melt, how happy they are. Thank you for trusting me with this mission. Love WHAXX.'

After the first stop, the boys fell asleep for most of the journey, and awoke just as we pulled into the hotel carpark. We needed to explore Savannah. We were situated in downtown known as the historic and Victorian district. Immediately noticeable to us was the slight change in climate, which was more humid and felt like the subtropical climates we were used to. It was easy to see it was the oldest city in the State of Georgia and seemed very colonial. Established in 1733 on the Savannah river, it became the British capital of the province of Georgia. Savanna has an historic past having been a strategic port in the American Revolution and the Civil War and today is an industrial centre and an important Atlantic sea port. The architecture with all the historic buildings was glorious as we walked through many of the twenty-two park like squares which, with cobblestones intact, felt as though we could have been in parts of London. Finding a café was easy as we were spoilt for choice and we spent a couple of hours eating and relaxing and generally people watching whilst the boys played in the park area.

Early the next day found us on the way to Washington. The story of the message in the bottle continued on and off throughout our journey, which took us through the Carolinas South and North and on to Virginia. It was a very long journey for all of us, approximately 575 miles, and we welcomed the sight of our hotel as it appeared on the road ahead. Needless to say, a good night's sleep was needed. The next day after breakfast, tired though we all were, we couldn't wait to become one of the millions of tourists who visit the capital of the United States each year. Confusion regarding the name needed clearing up. Washington DC named after George Washington and formally known as Washington District of Columbia. Often referred to as just DC, it is a federal district and is not in any State of America. There is a State in America called Washington, also named after the first president, but that is situated in the Pacific North West region. After that was cleared up the boys disappeared back into their rooms in search of their sunglasses, as it was a glorious clear sunny day and we then headed towards Capitol Hill. The sight of the Capitol building in the distance didn't disappoint – with its distinct white exterior in the neoclassical style it dominated the landscape. With both the Washington and Lincoln monuments lying to the west and the Supreme court and the Library of Congress to the East, the actual Capitol building is situated on Capitol Hill at the eastern end of Pennsylvania Ave.

The boys were appreciating Capitol Hill too, but from a different point of view. With their wraparound sunglasses they were getting into the character of two FBI agents covering each other's backs as they chased, turned and ran towards the Capitol Building with their index and middle fingers pointed as weapons. We could hear the odd few words of "GO, GO, GO" and "I've got your back, Bro".

Whilst the big chase was going on, Keith and I tried to piece together the US political terminologies ie, Congress, Senate, House of Representatives etc. We knew the Capitol building was the meeting place of the US Congress and that Congress is the elected group of politicians responsible for making laws and the Congress is made up of both the Senate and The House of Representatives. We later were able to focus a bit more as we learned that the Senate has two members from each State of the 50 States, a total of 100 members, and the numbers for The House of Representatives is based on the population from each State. California is the most populous and has 53 members. The total members have been fixed at 435. That was enough for one day and we were now ready for the White House. We decided to walk along Pennsylvania Avenue, which took us just over an hour before we arrived at number 1600, The White House. An amazing piece of Neo classical/Palladian architecture and very impressive. It was the first president George Washington who selected the site for the White House in 1791, and every president since

John Adams has occupied it, although there have been many renovations by previous Presidents since. We couldn't help but compare the official residence and workplace of the United States President with the official residence and workplace of the United Kingdom Prime Minister, which are worlds apart. The boys were peering through the railings trying hard to get a glimpse of The President or his wife, but unfortunately they were out of luck. I thankfully noticed that the railings were quite close together so it would be impossible for any child to get their heads stuck between them. We moved around to the back of the building and again peered through the railings, this time at the grounds. We understood The First Lady was promoting healthy eating habits and had developed an extensive vegetable garden and we were hoping to see her in her jeans and an old hat digging up some veg, but she didn't oblige – all we did see were her gardeners wearing old hats and jeans, digging and watering the area. Whilst we were there, in home schooling mode, we learnt some fun facts about the White House.

A former Prime Minister of the UK Winston Churchill whilst staying at the White House claimed he saw the Ghost of Abraham Lincoln when he emerged from the bathroom of Lincolns bedroom.

Painting the outside surface of the White House requires 570 gallons of paint.

There are 132 rooms, 35 bathrooms over 6 levels in the

residence, 412 doors, 147 windows, 28 fireplaces, 8 staircases, 3 elevators, and a movie theatre. There is an outside swimming pool, jogging track, putting green.

The White House kitchen is able to serve dinner to as many as 140 guests; it employs five full time chefs.

Known by other names such as Executive Mansion, Presidents House, Presidents Palace, it was President Theodore Roosevelt who changed the name to the White House in 1901.

The basement of the White House resembles a mini Mall with shops, including a chocolate shop. There is also a laundry and housekeeping is housed in the basement as well as a full size bowling alley.

Behind the West Wing a swimming pool is located built at the request of President Gerald Ford.

In 1933 President Franklin D. Roosevelt had an indoor pool built for use as therapy for his polio. President Nixon had the pool covered over and turned it into a press room.

During the Obama administration, a 2800 square foot vegetable garden was designed, producing up to 2000 pounds of fresh produce annually. This helped feed everyone from the Presidential family, staff, and the local soup kitchens.

Jimmy Carter had solar panels installed on the White House roof. Ronald Regan had them removed and in 2013 Obama re-installed them.

The first family are billed every month for their food. They do not pay for rent.

The famous West Wing that houses the Oval Office, Situation Room and Cabinet room was only intended as temporary.

It was a full fun-packed day, a bit exhausting but we were ready for the long walk back to the car. Our next destination, New York, sadly was really our last, at least for now.

The great reality of experiencing travelling and living the way we did was the fact that we were always in control of what happened next, including our next destination. It was exciting to have the freedom to change our minds if we so wished and at the same time it was an easy way to live, almost gentle on the mind. We knew this would have to end and it would be back to school, back to work and back to living in a house, but something was happening way beyond our control. We had been following the news of the ash cloud which was now bringing many flights and airports around the world to a complete standstill. We had been planning, in four days' time to head to Malta, which was to be our new home; however, due to the massive ash cloud disruption we had no idea when this was actually going to happen. We decided to put these thoughts to one side and enjoy our last destination, New York.

From DC it took as around four and a half hours driving at a leisurely pace, stopping now and again. We concluded the last Once upon a Time Story of the trip and the boys were getting excited, restless and couldn't wait to arrive in

New York. We drove through Baltimore on to Philadelphia and finally to Newark. This took us through the State of Maryland, Delaware and then on to New Jersey. The traffic was congested as expected as soon as we hit the outskirts of Newark. It was late afternoon when we arrived at the hotel and evening when we finally got settled with our enormous amount of luggage, and so all that was left for us to do was to hunt for a New York type of diner. The next day we headed for the Empire State Building. We were aware of the big drop in temperature, so our thick coats, hats and gloves were very useful. As we left the hotel we couldn't help but notice the rather large signs in the lobby advising that all flights out of Newark and JFK were cancelled until further notice. We took the train to Penn Station and headed for the west side of 5th Ave between west 33rd and 34th streets. I have often thought that the easiest way to get to know a city is to take one of the tourist open top buses but this is not necessary in Manhattan as it has a grid system which, seemingly complex at first, is actually simple and makes Manhattan immediately navigable. This certainly made the city welcoming for me who is without any sense of direction and so, with me taking charge of the route, we headed down towards 6th Ave towards West 34th St and on to 5th Ave. We were in midtown Manhattan, home to the Chrysler building as well as the Empire State Building, which didn't disappoint with all its Art Deco splendour. Dominating the area, the Empire State Building gives the impression that it's been there for ever comfortably fitting in with its surroundings. We were so happy to enter the building as the temperature seemed to be dropping fast. Whilst Keith was queuing for the tickets, we learnt a few facts about the building and its history.

Designed by William Lamb, it was the tallest building in the world between 1931 and 1972.

It was opened in 1931 by President Herbert Hoover who turned the lights on from Washington DC.

The name derived from the nickname for New York. The Empire State.

On a clear day from the observation deck you can see 5 States: New York, Pennsylvania, New Jersey, Massachusetts, and Connecticut.

The colour of the building's lights change according to seasonal or current events, for example on Valentine's Day the building is lit with red.

It took just 410 days to be constructed, which was ahead of schedule and also the final costs came in under budget.

Including the antenna spire, it is 1454 ft high.

It has 103 floors, and 6514 windows.

From street level to the 103rd floor there are 1,872 steps. An annual race is held to climb 1,576 steps.

Because there are so many businesses in the Empire State Building it has its own post code: 10118

The building has a lightning rod near the top which is

struck by lightning around 23 times a year.

The top of the building is used for broadcasting the majority of FM radio stations and commercial TV stations.

It is said, the Empire State Building makes more money from its ticket sales for its observation deck than it does from office rent.

It took a while after opening to rent all the offices in the building mainly due to the Great Depression and it was nicknamed "The Empty State Building". It wasn't until the 1950s that it became profitable.

In 1945 a B-25 Mitchell bomber crashed into the building due to extreme fog. The aircraft dived into the 78th and 79th floors. The pilot had become disorientated; he was on his way to La Guardia airport. The accident caused pieces of the bomber's engine to slice through one of the elevator shafts. A lady called Betty Lou was in one of the lift cars and survived the 75-storey plunge to the bottom. It is thought that more than 1000 feet of cable gathered at the bottom of the shaft helped to cushion the impact.

The event is still the longest elevator fall to boast a survivor and is listed in the Guinness Book of Records.

It is the most photographed building in the world.

Keith joined us, complete with tickets, and we headed for the queue for the elevator and the 86th floor Observation deck. I couldn't help it but the vision of Meg Ryan, Tom Hanks and the little boy were vivid in my mind as we stepped out of the elevator, assisted by a smiling attendant. The first thing we all noticed was the drop in temperature – it seemed freezing as we headed outside onto the deck and there was a cold wind, but it was well worth it. There is a full 360 degrees of Manhattan. WOW. Unfortunately for us it was not a clear day, but we managed to see most of Manhattan, The Rockefeller Center, Chrysler Building, Ground Zero World Trade Center site, Times Square, Statue of Liberty, Brooklyn Bridge, Central Park, and more. If it hadn't been for what felt at the time like freezing conditions we would have stayed a lot longer just soaking up the vista that lay before us, but enough was enough and we eventually headed down to the warmth of the gift shop, which was of course on the way out, designed for you to spend money on trinket souvenirs – which of course we did. I remember tall wooden puzzles of the Empire State being in the hands of the boys who couldn't wait to spend their pocket money, and there was Mum who just had to have one of the more sophisticated Empire State Building martini glasses, which still survives today. It was mid-afternoon when we eventually left the building and time to find a New York diner for some pastrami on rye. Afterwards we walked and walked around the streets and avenues taking in Macys, Maddison Square Gardens, Times Square and Broadway, and eventually headed back to the station. The boys were exhausted. Tomorrow was another day.

One of our favourite areas of Manhattan is undoubtably

SoHo and the Grenwich Village area, often called the Bohemian Capital, a trendy area on the West Side of Manhattan. So, the next day we made our way to a subway station close to the area and began walking. Without a grid system to rely on it was easy to get lost in this vicinity as we made our way through the labyrinth of named streets. The village itself was once a rural hamlet and not part of New York city, but today it fits in comfortably without any skyscrapers. We loved the brownstones and townhouses which date back to the 19th century, most of them now belonging to wealthy New Yorkers. On the corner of Bedford St and Grove St, at 90 Bedford is the exterior of the apartment used in the famous series Friends, although the main part of the series is shot in a Los Angeles studio. We made our way to MacDougal St and found ourselves spoilt for choice for bars, cafes and restaurants. After lunch we wandered into the SoHo area which is named after South of Houston (So Ho) to Canal St. Famous for its Art Galleries, Artists and loft Areas and its numerous upmarket boutiques. I remember wandering into one where live birds hung in and out of cages, champagne was free flowing and sculptures of old men were sitting on park benches amongst a sea of vintage clothing, truly an experience. It brought back memories to Keith and me of a purchase in SoHo years before of a Lennon sketch; however, unfortunately this time we never found the shop, which was probably a good thing as we saved a fortune. We wandered to Little Italy expecting to find the Godfather but we didn't which was a bit disappointing as there were few Italian restaurants. We also wandered into China Town which was a little bit more exciting, but having lived in Hong Kong for 15 years, it wasn't really comparable. The next day we planned to pay our respects to Ground Zero.

There was a feeling of calmness surrounding the area known at the time as Ground Zero. It was hard to imagine the reality of what had happened on September 11, 2001. Keith and I recalled the day as we had watched the news unfold on the TV as two terrorist aircraft flew into the north and south towers of The World Trade Center building causing massive damage and fires leading to the collapse of the 110 storey skyscrapers. The final count of deaths was 2977. At first it was difficult to realise that what we saw in front of us was not an American action movie. We were as shocked as the rest of the world and wondered what the next move would be. Josh wasn't born at that time and Jake was 17 months. Ground Zero was now being calmly and carefully rebuilt. We slowly moved on towards Wall St. Having enjoyed a long leisurely lunch amongst busy city types rushing through every mouthful of pastrami, we were glad we were just tourists in charge of our own time. Wall Street itself is an eight-block long street, famous as a financial district and home to the New York Stock Exchange and NASDAQ. (Global electronic marketplace dealing with securities.) In the small restaurant we could pick up on the pressures, and tensions and even the uneasiness of the patrons. It was great just to be tourists. We made our way back to the hotel as we needed to complete the final packing for our trip to Malta. First, however, we needed to check to see if we had a flight to catch as the news each day was about the closure of airports and flights round the world due to the ash cloud. Some time ago we had booked a flight from Newark to Munich with an Air Malta connection to Malta. We decided to go to the airport and check for ourselves. Lady luck certainly embraced us that day, as we were told that our flight to Munich was going to be the first out the following day and if we checked in immediately we would secure our seats. We were warned, however, that they were unable to confirm the connecting flight to Malta. We decided to risk it. We felt sorry for the people whose flights had been cancelled previously as they were told to wait until they could be fitted into a schedule which could mean an extra few days or more wait. On arrival at Munich we found that the Air Malta flight was cancelled but there might possibly be a flight to Catania in Sicily the next day. Catania was another step closer to Malta, so we decided to book it. Obviously because of all the disruption hotels were fully booked but we managed to find a small room at an extortionate price nearby and we all piled into it along with a ton of luggage. We managed to get on the Catania flight without a clue as to what to do when we arrived in Sicily, but we did know there were road and ferry routes to Malta. Lo and behold, Lady Luck struck again.

Halfway to Sicily the pilot announced that for operational reasons the aircraft was going on to Malta after Sicily and that anyone bound for Malta could stay on board, so after 10 months we landed at our new home.

I'm sure the future will hold many more adventures.

New York New York

The Capitol

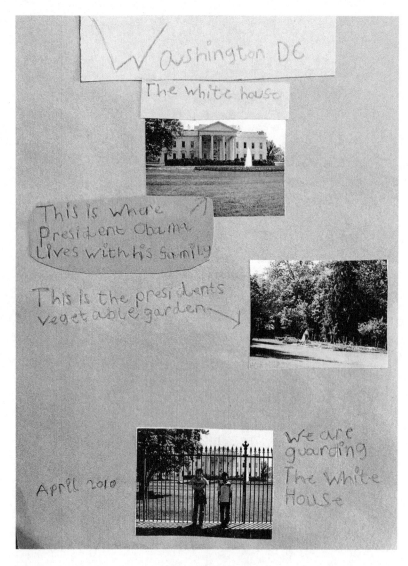

Washington DC

The white house

This is where President Obama Lives with his family

This is the presidents vegetable garden

We are guarding The White House

April 2010

The White House